TRADE TALKS WITH MEXICO: A TIME FOR REALISM

PETER MORICI

**NPA Committee on
Changing International Realities**

NATIONAL PLANNING ASSOCIATION

**TRADE TALKS WITH MEXICO:
A TIME FOR REALISM**

CIR Report #22
NPA Report #253

Price $15.00

ISBN 0-89068-110-4
Library of Congress
Catalog Card Number 91-62324

 C439

Contents

Trade Talks with Mexico: A Time for Realism
Peter Morici

Foreword

The National Planning Association's Committee on Changing International Realities is a unique network of senior business, labor and academic leaders who are interested in the impacts of globalization on the United States. This diversity is a key asset for the Committee; it has resulted in a strong research program and very interesting Committee meetings.

Because CIR members are from business, labor and the academic community, it is not reasonable to expect all on them to speak with one voice on a possible U.S.-Mexico free trade agreement. Some members believe that the benefits of such an agreement are greater than the costs, while other members believe that the costs of a U.S.-Mexico FTA are greater than any benefits.

However, most Committee members feel that many aspects of any new FTA are being glossed over in the public policy debate. Also, general information on and understanding of several FTA-related issues remain very low. For these reasons, the Committee has worked with Dr. Peter Morici, of the University of Maine and NPA, to produce this study. Not all Committee members agree with every point made in the study. Nevertheless, the Committee believes that this study can help all who are involved in the public policy process.

John J. Simone
Chair,
Committee on Changing International Realities

About the Author

Peter Morici is a Professor of Economics at the University of Maine and a Senior Fellow at the National Planning Association. Prior to joining the University, Dr. Morici was a Vice President at NPA. He received his Ph.D. from the State University of New York at Albany.

He is the author of seven books and many monographs and journal articles on international trade policy and North American economic integration. His most recent books are *Making Free Trade Work: The Canada-U.S. Agreement* (Council on Foreign Relations Press, 1990) and *Reassessing American Competitiveness* (National Planning Association, 1988). Later in 1991, *A New Special Relationship: The Free Trade Agreement and U.S.-Canada Commercial Relations* will be published jointly by the Institute for Research on Public Policy in Halifax and the Carleton University Centre for Trade Policy and Law in Ottawa.

Introduction

In September 1990, President Bush notified the Congress that he intended to negotiate a free trade agreement with Mexico. His action followed a formal request from President Salinas and a strong expression of interest from Prime Minister Mulroney to have Canada included in the talks. In June 1991, the House and Senate passed resolutions extending fast track negotiating authority. This established an early 1993 target for the conclusion of negotiations.[1]

For Mexico, a free trade agreement with the United States, perhaps including Canada, would mark the culmination of a radical change in national economic strategy. In the mid-1980s, Mexico turned away from decades of import substitution and domestic subsidies, which had left as their legacy an uncompetitive industrial structure, a burdensome debt and an institutionalized incapacity for self-sustaining growth. President Salinas is seeking to reorient the Mexican economy to respond to, rather than resist, international market signals and eliminate the need for protection.

For Mr. Salinas, the stakes are high in trade talks with the United States; rapid labor force growth, rising poverty and increasing demands for social and political progress require rapid economic growth. Without ever-expanding access to foreign markets—in particular, the rich U.S. market—his strategy is severely handicapped, perhaps doomed, and Mexico is in danger of slipping into permanent economic lethargy and political instability.

OPPORTUNITIES AND RISKS

For the United States and Canada, a true free trade agreement with Mexico—one eliminating tariffs, corralling quotas and reducing nontariff measures, and addressing services and investment—would be a big step, too. It would offer important opportunities but impose major risks. In negotiations, structuring an agreement that controls and manages these risks would be critical for ensuring that U.S. and Canadian benefits exceed costs. This is no easy challenge.

Proponents of free trade with Mexico argue that the benefits of free trade would be large and the adjustments imposed on labor minimal. Opponents have often portrayed free trade as a negative sum game with workers in all three countries losing. There is some truth in both arguments. Free trade with Mexico offers opportunities for economic gains through greater specialization but would impose significant costs on those workers and communities asked to move into new activities.[2]

This study attempts to offer a balanced view of the issues before us. It places the negotiations in the context of the competitive pressures acting on the United States, tensions in the multilateral trading system, Mexican economic reforms and prospects, and what role the U.S.-Canada Free Trade Agreement (FTA) might play.

The overall conclusions of the study are twofold, First, if there is going to be a free trade agreement with Mexico, then it must be structured in very specific ways to ensure that the benefits promised by proponents are realized and that the costs cited by opponents are minimized and decline over time.

Second, a free trade agreement with Mexico would not merely mean an extension of the evolving relationship between the United States and Canada. An agreement with Mexico that maximizes benefits and minimizes costs would have to be broader and deeper than the FTA. In the end, the three countries may have to evolve toward more of an economic community than a free trade area. In such a community, environmental and workplace standards, though independently set and enforced, are governed by a common floor, and the range of policies affecting trade with third countries becomes a somewhat more shared enterprise.

Benefits

Mexico offers a promising market for a wide range of U.S. and Canadian technology-intensive goods and skill-intensive services. For many U.S.-Canadian multinational corporations (MNCs), investment in Mexico, coupled with assured Mexican access to the U.S.-Canadian market, would offer the opportunity to counter wage and marketing advantages enjoyed by European Community (EC) and Japanese competitors by virtue of their proximity to Eastern Europe and East and Southeast Asia. Indeed, the dismantling of statist economic policies in Mexico offers the United States many of the same kinds of investment and trade opportunities that the collapse of socialism in Eastern Europe offers the EC and that the expansion of the *keiretsu* and other industrial networks in Asia offers Japan.

By combining inexpensive Mexican labor with U.S.-Canadian capital and technology, free trade offers the opportunity for more efficient continental specialization as capital and labor move to new pursuits in all three countries.

Costs

However, such transitions are never frictionless, and broadly based benefits in the United States would be paid for by disruptions in the lives of semiskilled workers employed in U.S. manufacturing, services and agriculture. Often these kinds of jobs make up a significant portion of the employment for whole communities—free trade would disrupt labor markets and impose hardships on these cities and towns.

Mexico's industrial wages are about at one-seventh of the level paid in the United States, and its labor force will continue to grow very rapidly through the beginning of the next century— nearly three-fifths of its 85 million people are under the age of 30. Consequently, free trade poses real threats to American workers in industries such as apparel, electrical and telecommunications equipment, and automotive products. The potential disruption to U.S. labor markets and in the lives of American workers cannot be dismissed as merely the "transitional" problems usually associated with trade liberalization. As the skill levels of Mexico's workers improve—and with an 80 percent literacy rate they will improve rapidly—the scope of U.S. activities challenged by Mexican workers will expand.

Proponents have argued that free trade would close the gap between Mexican and U.S. wages. However, this would be a long process. Consider the following. If a revaluation of the peso were to raise the current Mexican wage to 20 percent of U.S. levels and if Mexican real wage growth were to exceed U.S. wage growth by 4 percent a year indefinitely—two fairly heroic assumptions— Mexican wages would reach 40 percent of U.S. levels after 18 years and 80 percent in 36 years. It is interesting to note that in 1960 the compensation of the typical Japanese industrial worker stood at 10 percent of the U.S. level, and 36 years later it stood at 72 percent.[3] At the end of the 1980s, the wage levels in the four East Asian Tigers[4] had reached only about one-fifth of U.S. levels.

Although low Mexican wages must be placed in juxtaposition to low Mexican productivity, it is important to recognize that much of the low productivity in Mexico results from the use of outdated and inadequate capital and poor management in the traditional industrial sector. In the Maquiladora sector, where firms like Ford, General Electric and AT&T have invested in modern plants, Mexican productivity is respectable. In these plants, labor productivity is much higher than one-seventh of U.S. levels. The plants now account for about one-half of Mexico's merchandise exports. These plants, not the facilities farther south constructed during the import-substitution era, are representative of the kind of competition new Mexican exports offer.[5]

Proponents of free trade have pointed to the EC's success in absorbing Portugal and Spain—two very low wage economies. However, it is important to recognize that Mexico's population is 85 million—about 30 percent of the combined size of the United States and Canada. The comparable figures for Portugal and Spain are 50 million and 15 percent of the EC. Moreover, in joining the EC, Portugal and Spain became eligible for community-wide regional development programs and accepted EC-wide obligations regarding environmental and workplace health and safety standards, which are being established by the 1992 initiative. U.S. adjustment costs regarding free trade with Mexico cannot be dismissed as comparable in scope to the EC absorbing the Iberian nations.

REASONS FOR CAUTION

Quite apart from labor adjustment issues, the United States and Canada need to be cautious about how they approach free trade negotiations with Mexico. Although the FTA establishes the template for talks with Mexico, these negotiations will be no simple replay of the Canada-U.S. talks.

The FTA deepens and broadens the benefits, rights and protections that the United States and Canada enjoy in each other's market under the General Agreement on Tariffs and Trade by eliminating tariffs, addressing many nontariff barriers more rigorously than the GATT, extending the scope of nontariff policies addressed, and enforcing the agreement with fair, prompt and efficient dispute settlement features.

In the FTA, Canada and the United States have addressed or are committed to tackling bilaterally in follow-on negotiations many of the issues that proved very difficult in the Uruguay Round—notably agriculture, safeguards and adjustment, foreign investment regulations, procurement, subsidies and predatory pricing (dumping), product standards, and intellectual property. Also, they are taking on difficult sectoral issues—notably trade in energy products, automotive products, and business and financial services.

Aggressive progress in these areas was central to achieving a meaningful bilateral pact, and it would be critical to achieving a workable agreement with Mexico. Importantly, though, these issues were more tractable in a U.S.-Canadian context than in the GATT because the United States and Canada share so much in terms of their *legal and regulatory institutions, economic institutions and approaches to industrial policy*, levels of development and consequent *wage structures,* expectations for *environmental regulations* and *workplace health and safety standards.* In talks with Mexico, none of these conditions are present. The importance of this fundamental institutional reality should not be overlooked.

The reader is asked to consider five sets of issues. *First,* U.S., Canadian and Mexican negotiators will be beset by the complications of widely different, even if somewhat converging, *legal and regulatory systems,* greatly complicating the harmonization of government policies, practices and business regulations necessary to achieve an integrated North American market. If the United States, Canada and Mexico try to paper over these difficulties and do not harmonize their policy regimes, many of the long-term benefits of creating a single North American market will be lost.

Most of the significant barriers to international economic integration now emanate from domestic industrial policies. Without harmonization, each partner could practice employment and investment predation in the structuring of its domestic regimes. If one partner were much more aggressive in such a process, it could become a free rider in a trade agreement. As discussed in Chapter 6, the Mexican use of subsidies and a competition policy that has encouraged monopolies, "duopolies" and discrimination against foreign goods should be critical American and Canadian concerns in this regard.

Second, focusing on *economic institutions and industrial policy,* Mexican economic reforms, though impressive, still have many hurtles to clear. Although Mexico has taken important steps toward a market economy—in particular, lowering tariffs and eliminating most import quotas, easing foreign investment restrictions, and selling many parastatals[6]—it continues to have a significantly managed—overtly and covertly—economy. Mexico's regulation of private transactions (for example, in the automobile industry), remaining restrictions on foreign investment, and the range of activities reserved for state ownership are still well outside the norms of industrialized economies. What could emerge in Mexico is an aggressive application of Japanese-style market-responsive capitalism, in which Mexico's economy is increasingly alert to international market signals, but where the state plays a key role in helping the private and parastatal sectors identify and meet the challenges and opportunities offered by global and North American markets.

Also, although Mexico has embarked on some political reforms—e.g., broader representation in its Congress—progress in the political area lags economic liberalization. The potential for instability or a return to leftist government, more faithful to tenants of "the Revolution," are threats to economic reform that cannot be dismissed.

Mexico acceded to the GATT as a developing country, giving it some latitude to discriminate through sectoral policies. However, it is important to remember that Mexico is the fifth largest exporter of manufactures among developing countries, ranking only behind the four East Asian newly industrializing countries (NICs). The United States would hardly find the conduct of industrial policy, still the norm in Mexico, acceptable in shaping a trade agreement with Korea. Yet, Mexican exports to the United States exceed those of Hong Kong, South Korea, Taiwan, and Singapore.

Nevertheless, Mexico, along with Chile, has been at the forefront of Latin American economic reform, almost exceeding U.S. aspirations in the pace with which it has been disassembling the bulwarks of statism and protectionism. U.S. recognition of these efforts is essential for President Salinas to have the economic and political resources to continue the process and to foster sorely needed political reforms. In shaping and implementing American responses, either excessive enthusiasm or perceived indifference toward President Salinas' efforts could diminish momentum for additional liberalization in Mexico.

Striking a balance is difficult because political considerations play a considerable role in U.S. economic policy toward Mexico. Simply put, the United States cannot afford to let the economic reforms in Mexico fail, as the security consequences of instability there are unacceptable. Herein lies a danger for the United States. It could respond to Mexican aspirations with a quick deal that helps shore up President Salinas' immediate political situation but fails to provide the foundation for a longer-term, more comprehensive progress. By the end of the 1990s, the cumulative benefits accruing to both Mexico and the United States could be much smaller than might be attainable ultimately through a more deliberative approach.

It behooves U.S., Canadian and Mexican officials to recognize one of the more powerful lessons of the Canada-U.S. negotiations. Fast track negotiations are only the first step—they result in broad commitments and goals. Ultimately, after they are signed, modern free trade agreements, such as the FTA, engage their participants in processes of parallel actions and continuous negotiations in which concessions are exchanged over many years. If, out of enthusiasm for recent Mexican reforms or political haste, American officials get out in front of their Mexican counterparts in making concessions, Mexico could lose important incentives to address some of the most difficult issues—e.g., constitutional, statutory and institutional issues regarding services, investment, energy, intellectual property, import measures, and various business regulations. For the United States, the balance of benefits to costs could easily become negative, and the distributional consequences in labor markets could easily erode American political resolve to assist Mexico further down the road.

Third, the opportunity of combining North American capital and technology with the Mexican wage structure offers the possibility of greatly enhancing the *cost competitiveness* of many North American MNCs. With U.S. and Canadian firms investing heavily in Mexico, the United States and Canada could exchange high-technology/skilled manufactures (especially producer durables and sophisticated components) and services for low-technology/skilled manufactures. In the process, advocates of free trade say the United States and Canada would gain high-wage jobs and lose low-wage jobs. However, the numbers of jobs may not balance out in the short run or even in the long run, and many displaced workers may not have the skills required for new employment opportunities.

So far, the United States has benefited most among industrialized countries from reforms in Mexico. As Japanese and European investors have stayed on the sidelines, U.S. companies have rushed to take advantage of economic liberalization in Mexico. Offshore investors have been concerned that Mexican reforms may not be adequately institutionalized (permanent) and that the United States could close its markets by invoking anti-dumping and other trade remedy laws. A key motivation for Mexico in seeking free trade is to assuage both sets of concerns.

As discussed in Chapter 2, after free trade institutionalizes Mexican economic reforms, Japanese and European MNCs—having better access to skilled labor, technology and capital than American and Canadian firms—may be in a better position to exploit new opportunities in Mexico than U.S. and Canadian MNCs. As a result, patterns of Mexican purchases of capital goods and services, which are now decidedly oriented toward the United States, could shift somewhat toward Japan and Europe.

This reveals a basic problem for the United States and Canada in talks with Mexico. Mexico is undertaking reforms that open its market multilaterally to trade and investment, while it is seeking, as recognition, preferential access to the U.S. and Canadian markets.

In the end, the increase in Mexican sales of low-technology/skilled manufactures and services to the United States and

Canada may not be matched by an equal increase in Mexican purchases of high-technology/skilled goods from its northern neighbors, as Mexico purchases of producer durables, components and services shift toward the traditional suppliers of Japanese and EC MNCs in Asia and Europe. The resulting North-South exchange of goods, services and jobs could turn out to be unbalanced and disappointing from a U.S. and Canadian perspective.

Economists would argue that exchange rate and other "market adjustments" would correct the resulting growth in the overall U.S. trade deficits.[7] However, as discussed in Chapter 4, these market adjustments would add to the effects of other, nontrade-related trends that are already placing downward pressure on the living standards of younger American industrial workers. While economists and proponents of free trade can counter that these are the fortunes of open competition, they should pause to consider the political consequences of such a dynamic for their long-term goal of full integration of the U.S., Canadian and Mexican economies.

As already noted, a trade agreement would require many years to implement and continuous negotiations. To be successful, to keep the bicycle of liberalization moving lest we fall off, such a process would require political support in the Congress and the Parliament long after an agreement was signed and the process begun. An agreement that does contain adequate transitional mechanisms and safeguards for semiskilled workers but does not assure an exchange of preferential access between the United States/Canada and Mexico would be subject to continuous political attack. In the end, support for continued liberalization could dissolve.

Fourth, lax environmental enforcement and poor workplace safety conditions in Mexico played an important role in the congressional debate regarding approval of presidential negotiating authority. Together, these issues raise fundamental questions. What should be required to ensure fairness to workers in all three countries? How far should trilateral trade negotiations, or any trade negotiations, pry into domestic policy prerogatives? Should the negotiations, like the Uruguay Round of multilateral trade negotiations and talks leading to the Canada-U.S. Free Trade Agreement, exclude environmental and workplace health and safety standards, or like the EC 1992 process include them?

These questions should be put in the context of evolving U.S. objectives for the multilateral system, the impact of trade negotiations on national sovereignty, and the special challenges posed by regional trade agreements.

At its core, U.S. trade policy is built around the premise that trade flows should be driven by market forces—what economists call comparative advantages. Its own transgressions notwithstanding, the United States has sought to establish an ever-expanding GATT framework that defines market-consistent policies and then constrains nations to pursue policies consistent with these concepts.

With the increasing international integration of economies, the effective pursuit of a market-driven framework for trade has impelled the United States to broaden its goals for the GATT to include nontariff instruments of policy that in the past were considered firmly within the domain of domestic policy. These include, for example, product standards, the application of domestic subsidies and countervailing duties, and the regulation of business and financial services. Trade has become so important to modern economies that virtually all domestic policies affect trade, and most now seem up for grabs in trade negotiations.

It is important to be clear that all international agreements have penetrated sovereignty. Setting tariffs is as much a sovereign act as specifying product standards or offering subsidies. Constraints on these sovereign powers are the price that national governments have accepted to obtain the benefits of greater foreign market access and specialization among countries. The scope of sovereign prerogatives open to negotiations has broadened as lower tariffs and improvements in transportation and communication technologies have expanded the opportunities for trade.

How far should the process go? The answer lies in the proximity of negotiating parities and the context in which they negotiate. For example, harmonizing product standards, or even making them more compatible and transparent, between France and Brazil, bilaterally and outside the GATT, would impose costs that far outweigh the benefits—the two countries are too far apart and just do not trade enough to warrant the costs.

In the context of the GATT, though, France, Brazil and many other countries are together seeking to make product standards more compatible and transparent. The 104-nation body is not seeking complete harmonization of standards—the diversity of GATT participants makes such a process impractical and too costly given the potential benefits. Instead, in the GATT, participants are seeking to circumscribe the way standards are made and enforced so that national differences do not pose unnecessary barriers to trade.

In the context of the EC, however, France and other European nations have discovered that the process should go beyond the GATT agenda to include, where possible, more harmonized product standards—the costs are lower and the benefits of a unified regional market are great.

Focusing on environmental and workplace safety enforcement, these are difficult to address effectively in the GATT, but in the EC 1992 process, participating nations found it essential to deal with them to ensure a level playing field within a single European market.[8]

The bottom line is that there are no hard and fast rules as to how deeply trade agreements should cut into national policymaking prerogatives. Participants need to define the agenda in terms and ways that ensure maximum and balanced benefits.

Environmental and workplace safety were not issues in the U.S.-Canada FTA talks because U.S. and Canadian environmental and workplace health and safety rules were already quite similar. Differences in standards and enforcement are too small to have an appreciable effect on bilateral trade and the competition for plants and jobs. However, inadequate enforcement of environmental and workplace standards in Mexico places U.S. and Canadian communities and workers at cost disadvantages vis-a-vis their Mexican counterparts. Lax enforcement in Mexico's Maquiladora sector has had effects much like locational subsidies that have been so important in industrial predation in other contexts.

Therefore, the economic logic for engaging Mexico in discussions of environmental and workplace issues, either directly in trade negotiations or through parallel discussions, is strong. It would be no more and no less an affront to Mexican sovereignty than for Mexico to seek fair application of U.S. and Canadian subsidy/countervailing laws and other trade remedy laws.

Fifth, progress in the GATT and the maintenance and expansion of a liberal trading system remain primarily dependent on *American leadership*. The United States should give careful consideration to how an agreement with Mexico could affect its multilateral goals.

In regional trade agreements, the vehicle traditionally used to ensure preferential access, and in turn balance-of-market opportunities, has been rules of origin. As discussed in Chapter 4, it is unlikely that this would prove effective in a trade agreement with Mexico. Alternatives, such as seeking preferred status for U.S. and Canadian MNCs under Mexico's foreign investment regulations, fly in the face of the most-favored-nation (MFN) principle.

The MFN principle is a fundamental element of the GATT and has already been dealt significant blows, for example, by implementation of the Tokyo Round codes and certain elements of the EC 1992 program. It may well be that the integrated regional trading bloc will replace the nation as the principal negotiating unit in the GATT and that a formalized and recognized two-tier application of the MFN principle—i.e., stronger obligations to bloc members than to other GATT members—becomes a standard feature of U.S., Japanese and EC-member policies.[9] This may or may not serve U.S. interests; however, we should know what we are doing when we do it, and understand its ramifications.

A free trade agreement with Mexico would implicitly, yet concretely, limit access to U.S. and Canadian markets for other developing countries. Also, to dampen domestic opposition to low-wage competition from Mexico, Washington and Ottawa could be forced to tighten restrictions on imports from other Latin American and Asian economies. This would run counter to President Bush's Enterprise for the Americas program, and trade relations with East and Southeast Asia could also suffer.

SUMMING UP: REASONS FOR AND AGAINST AN AGREEMENT

Political Realities

During the spring 1991 congressional debate on fast track negotiating authority, important economic reasons were offered for responding positively to Mexico's request for negotiations, and sound arguments were offered for not moving forward without a clear understanding of what free trade would entail. These considerations notwithstanding, it is clear that the Bush Administration is motivated by geopolitical concerns as well as economic considerations. Equally significant, in all three countries domestic policies would be central in implementing and further articulating any agreement initialed before fast track authority expires in May 1993.

The hard reality is that the United States has an enormous stake in social progress and stability in Mexico, and the Bush Administration's decision to negotiate a free trade agreement is colored by its desire to support economic and political reform there.

Other Ways to Help Mexico

Certainly, there are ways other than a free trade agreement to help Mexico—notably more substantial development aid and cooperative arrangements to ensure adequate resources and enforcement in the areas of sanitation and public utilities, transportation infrastructure, environmental protection, workplace safety, and improved income distribution. Mexico believes that it needs wider and more assured access to the U.S. market to transform its economy, Presidents Bush and Salinas believe a free trade agreement is the best way to achieve this, and Prime Minister Mulroney does not want Canada to be the odd man out.

This said, it is useful to review the arguments for and against free trade, as they point to the kinds of provisions that would be required in an agreement to ensure that the full benefits would materialize and the risks to American and Canadian workers would be limited. Without these provisions, the efficacy of a free trade agreement becomes highly questionable.

Factors Favoring an Agreement

A *comprehensive* free trade agreement would offer the United States, Canada and Mexico the opportunity to achieve a more efficient allocation of resources and raise their growth rates. If *properly structured*, it would offer both the United States/Canada and Mexico access to much expanded markets and encourage considerable new investment in North America to satisfy those market opportunities. Overall, free trade would make the North American economy better able to compete with the established and emerging centers of industrial activity in East and Southeast Asia and Europe. Moreover, as discussed in Chapter 7, a North American accord could increase the negotiating clout of the United States in the GATT.

Factors Against an Agreement

Emphasis is purposely placed on the words "comprehensive" and "properly structured" trade agreement. A conventional free trade agreement, for example one modeled after the U.S.-Israeli agreement or even the U.S.-Canada FTA, would not provide adequate transitional provisions to ensure that labor adjustments were controlled and minimized and that the long-term processes of liberalization and negotiations set in motion by an initial agreement would have the sustained political support necessary to succeed.

A conventional trade agreement would not address the problems created by the differences between U.S.-Canadian and Mexican wages, legal and economic institutions, U.S. and Canadian vulnerability to Japanese and European MNCs using Mexico as a back door to the affluent North American markets, or lax Mexican environmental and workplace health and safety enforcement. These are tractable problems; however, it is not at all clear that the three governments or their negotiators have recognized the scope of these problems or that they are prepared to fashion an agreement that adequately addresses them.

If a Deal, Then What Kind?

Negotiators from all three countries need to recognize that it serves their common interests to frame mechanisms that manage the adjustment process for semiskilled labor in the United States and Canada and for workers employed in the traditional Mexican manufacturing sector.

As discussed in Chapter 6, this could be achieved by pacing the growth of U.S. and Canadian duty free imports from Mexico in selected industries and vice versa. In sectors such as apparel, limiting the growth of the market shares of duty free imports to a negotiated "G" percent a year would ensure that adjustments are phased in slowly.

Much the same can be said about fashioning an agreement that gives the United States and Canada preferential market opportunities in Mexico comparable to those afforded Mexico in the United States and Canada.

Also, framing an agreement that requires Mexico, within agreed upon time frames, to conform its policies regarding subsidies, antitrust, intellectual property, foreign investment, and other industrial policies to the norms of Western industrialized countries would memorialize President Salinas's economic reforms and serve to more adequately ensure the United States and Canada a level playing field in North America.

Further, cooperative arrangements to bring environmental and workplace safety enforcement in Mexico closer to the standards adhered to in the United States and Canada would offer Mexicans a better life and U.S./Canadian workers a larger measure of fairness in their competition with Mexicans for jobs. As argued in Chapter 6, placing such efforts within the structure of an agreement or in a parallel accord could ensure that the technical support and funding is in place to achieve these objectives.

OUTLINE OF THE STUDY

The study that follows is divided into six chapters. Chapter 2 briefly examines the global forces acting on the North American economies, the Mexican economy and Mexican economic reforms. Chapter 3 reviews U.S. and Canadian commercial relations with Mexico. It provides background on existing trade agreements, barriers to trade and trade flows. Chapter 4 assesses the origins and scope of adjustments that would be imposed by free trade. Chapter 5 examines the role that the Canada-U.S. FTA should be given in establishing U.S. goals regarding Mexico. Chapter 6 analyzes some of the specific negotiating issues. Chapter 7 discusses the issues that free trade raises for the management of U.S. trade policy.

NOTES

1. Fast track authority expires May 31, 1993, and Mexico will choose a successor to President Salinas later that year.

2. It is important to remember that free trade creates economic gains by encouraging specialization, reallocating resources and essentially moving labor and capital to new pursuits in each country. In such a process, there are always losers—those whose incomes fall and those who endure periods of prolonged unemployment.

3. By the end of the 1980s, Japanese workers had reached approximate parity with U.S. workers.

4. Hong Kong, South Korea, Taiwan, and Singapore.

5. It is important to remember that arguments about low productivity were offered to assuage concerns about low wages in the Orient in the 1970s—productivity in newly industrializing countries quickly improves with the arrival of industrialized country capital and management, and productivity on export platforms usually far exceeds productivity in the indigenous industrial sector.

6. The term parastatal is used here to refer to entities owned or controlled by the government.

7. Events in the 1980s showed that there can be many real world complications in this process.

8. The notion of a common floor under workplace standards is often called the "social charter" or "social dimension" and refers to efforts to harmonize EC member states' policies on labor markets, occupational health and safety, social welfare, and social security.

9. The MFN principle was first conceived to apply to tariffs. Certainly, members of a simple free trade area or customs union apply two-tier MFN with regard to tariffs. However, since at least the Tokyo Round, the concept also has been used to describe and analyze the preferential treatment nations afford each other through the whole panoply of nontariff measures affecting trade. In the FTA, the United States and Canada engage in two-tier tariff MFN, something the GATT sanctions for free trade areas. The critical question then becomes how far does discrimination penetrate into nontariff areas. It is in this second sense that the term is used in this study.

Economic Reform in Mexico

2

Economic and political reform in Mexico confronts American policymakers with vexing challenges. In the context of Mexico's request for a bilateral trade agreement, the pace of reform will aggravate certain contradictions in U.S. foreign economic policy and, in the end, may force the United States to make difficult choices about its role in the multilateral trading system. This may be best appreciated in the context of some of the changes under way in the global economy and multilateral trading system that are inspiring Mexican reforms and bilateral initiatives.

THE GLOBAL CONTEXT

In the 1980s, Americans witnessed major victories of two long championed ideals—the dual triumphs of democratic institutions in Latin America and Eastern Europe and the increased acceptance of the notion that the mandates of markets, not governments, should guide the allocation of resources and development of national economies.

Focusing on the latter, the idea that national economic policies should be in step with the opportunities offered by international markets—lest they impose burdensome costs on national living standards—has gained considerable support.

In Western Europe, much of the motivation behind the EC 1992 program was to bring down the barriers to intra-European specialization that were impeding the ability of firms there to spread costs and achieve economies of scale.

In Latin America, governments faced with mounting debt problems have gone beyond macroeconomic remedies and have taken substantial steps to liberalize their economies. Economic reforms have made their economies more open to trade and investment and have sought to move the locus of economic decisionmaking from government ministries to private businesses. As shown in Table 1, Mexico and Chile have led in reforming their tax systems and exchange rate regimes, opening to direct foreign investment, privatizing parastatal corporations and generally reducing the reach of government regulation into many aspects of the everyday management of businesses.

This trend toward more "market-oriented" policies has not translated into much success in efforts to open commerce among the three major players in the GATT system—the United States, the EC and Japan—or between them and developing countries

15

TABLE 1
MICRO POLICY REFORMS IN MAJOR
LATIN AMERICAN ECONOMIES, 1980s

	Tax Reform	Financial Liberali- zation	Competitive Exchange Rate	Trade Liberali- zation	Foreign Investment Regulations	Priviti- zation	Deregu- lation
Mexico	++	0	+	++	++	++	+
Argentina	0	0	+	0	+	+	+
Brazil	+	0	+	0	−	+	−
Chile	+	++	++	++	+	++	+

Source: "Latin America in the 1980s," *International Economic Insight* (November/December 1990), p. 15.

outside their traditional regions of interest.[1] Most progress on the trade front appears to be regional in scope—e.g., the completion of the internal market in the EC, the FTA and the rapidly expanding scope of Japanese trade with East and Southeast Asia. This in no small measure results from considerable disagreement among the principal players about what constitutes market-oriented policies,[2] as well as the greater scope of adjustments that would be imposed by multilateral, as opposed to regional, liberalization.

For the purpose of interpreting the meaning of the changes taking place in Mexico, it is important to remain aware that the global movement toward more market-oriented policies does not necessarily represent an international embrace of the American vision of market capitalism—one steeped in Smithian notions of laissez-faire, as frequently espoused by Bush Administration economic advisors. Among the major players in the international trading system, there are many views about the appropriate roles for government. In particular, the idea that governments may at once respect the mandates of international markets and assist private businesses in identifying and responding to latent and apparent competitive opportunities remains ingrained in European and Japanese thinking and has gained currency among many members of Congress, business leaders, and respected American economists and other intellectuals.

This is why it is not hypocritical for the United States, the EC and Japan to advocate multilateral, bilateral and regional rules that support market-determined patterns of trade, while disagreeing so violently as to how that should be translated into the hard specifics of disciplines for subsidies, government procurement and conduct of domestic competition policy.

In shaping trade, investment and industrial policy, Mexican leaders should not be expected to be blind to these divergent views; Americans should recognize that current actions are governed by two important realities. First, Mexico is now engaged in a process of dismantling institutions, policies and practices that fundamentally resisted, indeed dismissed, the mandates of international markets and the opportunities offered by comparative advantage, trade and specialization. During the 1970s and early 1980s, these imposed significant economic inefficiency and hardship on the Mexican people. As much as in Eastern Europe, radical surgery is needed to redirect the processes of economic decisionmaking.

Second, the Salinas Administration clearly recognizes that Mexico, in the current international negotiating environment, will find its only real opportunity to gain substantial increased access to a major industrialized market in the United States. Therefore, it is not surprising that Mexico's reform process looks like a religious conversion to American-style strict laissez-faire principles. However, with Mexico's long tradition of the government playing "Rector" to the domestic economy,[3] we should not be surprised to see Mexico, where it can, adopting industrial policies that its leaders believe will help it exploit market opportunities ignored by the old import-substitution regime. In this way, Mexican approaches to industrial policy would be more consistent with Japanese and European models of market-oriented policies that emphasize government-corporate partnership. Automobiles and electronics seem like prime candidates for such approaches. Mexico has long records of intervention in these sectors and could look to Japan for new sources of capital and technology, as well as new guidance in shaping supportive government policies.

Also, the Mexican challenge emerges for the United States at a time when it may be least able to accept it. American advocates of multilateral and regional trade liberalization argue that freer trade would allow the United States to exchange production in low-technology/skilled industries for new production in high-technology/skilled industries.

The critical assumption is that the United States, with its vast system of public education and R&D infrastructure, has an enduring comparative advantage in the design of technologically sophisticated products and application of advanced manufacturing technologies. Belying this view is increasing evidence that the quality of the U.S. labor force, especially young entrants, has slipped.

Unlike young workers in Japan and Western Europe, most U.S. workers entering the labor force directly from high school do not have the requisite skills to work in a technologically sophisticated environment and are unlikely to obtain the necessary additional training. They do not have the skills needed to use technology in ways that will permit them to both earn high wages and be competitive in international markets.[4]

In evidence of this phenomenon, the Commission on the Skills of the American Workforce found that many employers are coping by deskilling jobs. When faced with competition from low-wage imports and shortages of skilled workers, they balk at installing the most advanced manufacturing technologies; frequently, they turn to third world production techniques, relying on transitory workers and low wages to remain competitive.[5]

Moreover, thanks in no small measure to the large U.S. budget deficits of the past decade and high Japanese savings rates, Japan has enjoyed very large current account surpluses. Therefore, compared to U.S. firms, Japanese firms are often in a much better financial position to expand facilities in Mexico and elsewhere; they enjoy an edge over and above the advantages they would be expected to have as a result of their industrial achievements.[6]

Under free trade, the United States would import from Mexico more products such as textiles and apparel, metal products, automotive products, consumer electronics, and telecommunications equipment, and it could export to Mexico some of the same in higher valued added categories. However, the real success of free trade for the United States would hinge on its ability to capitalize on the modernization of Mexican industry through sales of producer durables, sophisticated components and manufacturing-consulting, construction and engineering, financial, and business services that would be needed to create new competitive facilities in Mexico.

A trade agreement with Mexico might not result in such a balanced growth in trade if the United States affords Mexico preferential access to its market for low-technology/skilled products while Mexico liberalizes its trade and investment regimes to all comers. Armed with more capital and better technology, Japanese firms could establish production facilities that export low-wage products to the United States and purchase the sophisticated goods and services needed to make them in Japan and elsewhere in Asia.

As discussed in Chapters 5 and 6, the United States would be confronted with some tough choices. Rules of origin will not suffice to ensure the United States preferential access and adequate market opportunities in Mexico, and other steps it may take would compromise U.S. support for the MFN principle, which is central to the GATT.

THE MEXICAN ECONOMY

Mexico is a country with vast, but largely unfulfilled, potential.[7] With a population of about 85 million, it ranks 11th in world population. More important, Mexico's literacy rate exceeds 80 percent, and 59 percent of its people are younger than 30 years. These factors give the country a young, capable and rapidly growing labor force of about 27 million. In 1990, the United States exported $28 billion to Mexico, making it the third largest customer for U.S. products.

The Old Regime

During the postwar period, the Mexican economy grew rapidly. From the mid-1940s to the early 1970s, annual GDP growth averaged a brisk 6.7 percent, outpacing population growth by more than 3 percentage points a year. Macroeconomic policy was fiscally conservative by contemporary standards, and inflation averaged only 3.8 percent. In contrast, microeconomic policy—trade and industrial policy—was highly interventionist; like many Latin American countries, Mexico sought to industrialize through "import substitution" rather than exploitation of comparative advantages through specialization, export promotion and trade. Also, owing to long-held fears of foreign domination, foreign investment was discouraged and highly controlled.

During the early postwar decades, the import-substitution approach enjoyed considerable respectability among many prominent mainstream economic development specialists.[8] In the case of Mexico, as the statistics cited above indicate, this strategy worked quite well from the close of World War II through the early 1970s.

The dramatic increase in oil prices and the growth in Mexican export revenues that followed the 1973 OPEC embargo gave Mexican officials what they perceived to be the opportunity to pursue these policies with even greater vigor. The public sector overreach that followed ultimately precipitated an economic crisis and a radical change in policy.

The Setting. It is important to remember that the 1917 Mexican Constitution reserves a dominant role for the government in managing and regulating the national economy. The federal government is the institutionalization of the revolution, with the major unions, government employees and farmers allocated representation in the governing party—the Institutional Revolutionary Party (PRI).

Mexicans expect their government not to leave the determination of the overall course and pattern of economic development to private decisions. They expect their government to protect them from foreign economic domination and to ensure fairness—such as by limiting the rights of foreign corporations operating on their soil and by rigorously regulating the employment contracts between workers and businesses (discussed below).

Therefore, the federal government is entrusted with and expected to play a significant role in managing the economy. Mexicans call this role "Rector." This is cultural affectation and is not merely a matter of policy. For Americans negotiating with Mexicans, at either the official or private level, an understanding of this orientation is essential.

Prior to reforms that began in the mid-1980s, the government expressed this role of Rector through highly autarkic, inward-looking policies; these were often wrapped in a kind of revolutionary rhetoric that created the air of an Eastern European regime. Indeed, although Mexico was nominally a mixed-market economy, much of the private sector—and many private transactions—were explicitly or implicitly regulated by government agencies or through the purchases and sales of parastatal enterprises.

Until the 1970s, the parastatal sector was large by U.S. standards, but outside the resource sector, utilities and transportation, it was still quite small.[9] The bureaucracy in Mexico City sought to direct and manage economic development by regulating prices, product specifications and credit, and by offering various incentives and disincentives. It was not until the 1970s that government ownership expanded rapidly in terms of the share of GNP and scope of activities. By 1983, the parastatal sector produced about 18 percent of GDP.[10]

Trade Policy. Tariffs averaging 24 percent and a variety of other nontariff measures were employed to encourage domestic manufacturing and agriculture. These measures were structured to limit or prohibit imports for which domestic substitutes were available, while ensuring supplies of foreign components and machinery not available in Mexico. Among the measures were an elaborate system of import licensing, covering virtually all customs categories, and a reference price system that established arbitrarily high customs values for nearly one-quarter of all customs categories. On the export side, Mexico aggressively subsidized with direct aids such as preferential export financing, tax rebates and credits, and preferential energy prices (e.g., petrochemicals). In addition, Mexico used domestic production subsidies, domestic content and other aggressive performance requirements for foreign investors, and domestic working and exporting requirements for patents.[11]

Regulation. Government regulation touched virtually every sector of the economy. For example, freight regulations limited truckers to 1 of 11 regions and had the effect of creating cartel-like regional service centers that allocated shipments—these regulations had the effect of increasing the transportation costs on imported goods by about 15 percent; restrictive packaging and labeling standards, such as regulations specifying the materials to be used, raised the cost of containers by as much as 20 percent; automakers were limited in the number of models and lines they could manufacture; the government set insurance rates and did not permit rate competition; and similar inefficiencies were imposed by cumbersome restrictions and subsidies to parastatal firms in agriculture and food processing, fishing and other activities.

Foreign Investment Policy. Mexican policies toward foreign investment are best appreciated in a historical context. The industrialization strategy of the administration of Porfirio Diaz (1876-1910) strongly encouraged foreign investment in mining, basic industries and utilities. Growing resentment of foreign influence resulted in the classic lament: "Mexico, mother of foreigners, stepfather to Mexicans." During the revolutionary period (1910-25), a backlash against foreign investment emerged, and until the mid-1980s, foreign direct investment was discouraged. External capital requirements were largely met by borrowing.

Article 27 of the 1917 Constitution reserves to Mexicans all subsoil rights. Although foreigners may own land, the article establishes the constitutional basis for restricting (prohibiting) the sale of mineral rights to them. Foreigners may not own land within 100 kilometers of the country's borders or within 50 kilometers of the coastline (the "Restricted Zone").[12]

From 1917 to 1973, various decrees defined the scope of restrictions on foreign investment required by, or consistent with, the Constitution. These were embodied in the 1973 Law to Promote Mexican Investment and Regulate Foreign Investment (LFI). Prior to 1940, most foreign agricultural holdings were expropriated, and foreign-owned railways and the oil industry were nationalized. A 1944 decree established the Secretariat of Foreign Relations. Foreigners were required to obtain its permission to purchase controlling interests in agriculture, forestry, mining, real estate, and general industrial and commercial enterprises. In 1945, the Secretariat established the following areas as being limited to 49 percent foreign ownership: radio, film, fishing, advertising, and domestic air and highway transportation. Bottling and rubber were added to the list in 1947, timber in 1960 and mining in 1961.[13] In 1965, foreign participation in financial services was limited, and after 1970, permits were required for all foreign purchases and expansion in steel, cement, glass fertilizers, paper, and aluminum.

The 1973 LFI and subsequent decrees consolidated and extended this regime. Investment was divided into four areas.

a. Activities reserved to the state—extracting and refining of petroleum and natural gas; basic petrochemical production; mining and processing of radioactive minerals; certain other mining activities; generation and transmission of electricity; telegraphic communications; railroads; banks,[14] funds and financial trusts; and other activities that may be specified by law or regulation.

b. Activities reserved to Mexicans—broadcasting; urban and interurban automotive transportation; domestic air and maritime transportation (including coastal and high-seas towing); forestry; retail liquid gas distribution; stockbrokerages, stock exchange investment companies, bond and insurance institutions, and independent pension funds; and other activities that may be specified by law or regulation.

c. Activities subject to specific limitations—mining of coal, iron ore, phosphoric rock and sulfur (34 percent); secondary petrochemicals, and automotive parts (40 percent); and other activities that may be specified by law or regulation.

d. All other activities were limited to not more than 49 percent of foreign ownership.

All foreign investors were required to register with the National Registry of Foreign Investments.

The National Foreign Investment Commission (CNIE) applied these rules and was free to raise limits on foreign participation where deemed beneficial to the economy. Applications for foreign participation greater than 49 percent were subject to administrative review. Investments were screened to determine if they would displace domestic suppliers, expand exports, increase employment, source local components, and transfer technology. Many firms in the electronics, automotive and pharmaceuticals sectors were wholly foreign owned, but their activities were highly regulated in the context of sectoral development policies. One hundred percent foreign investment was permitted in the Maquiladoras.

Administrative review by CNIE was cumbersome, time consuming and not particularly transparent.

Parastatal Enterprises. The 1917 Constitution, the LFI and their interpretation through various decrees reserve certain "strategic sectors" to state ownership. However, some entities in virtually every sector of the economy came to be government owned as Mexican administrations sought to rescue insolvent companies to maintain employment, sustain supplies of items deemed essential and replace imports. During the 1970s, Mexican governments, flush with optimism from new-found oil wealth, used borrowed monies to purchase and subsidize parastatals. The number of entities in which Mexico City had an interest increased more than threefold to about 1,200. In the words of one Mexican diplomat speaking to a public gathering in New York recently, "You name it, we had it, steel mills, cabarets. . . ."[15]

Intellectual Property. Historically, Mexican protection of intellectual property has been weak. In 1987, amendments were made to the 1976 Law of Inventions and Trademarks (LIT); these resulted in some additional patent, trademark and trade secret protection, but in many areas the reforms were either inadequate or postponed until 1997.

For example, Mexican patent protection is for 14 years (10 years under the original 1976 law) compared to 17 years in the United States. Under the 1987 amendments, biotechnological and genetic processes, chemicals, medicines, beverages, food for animal consumption, fertilizers, pesticides, herbicides, and fungicides are withheld patent protection until 1997. Mexican law requires compulsory licensing if a patent is not worked domestically or used for export purposes—no such provisions exist in U.S. law. In addition, the Mexican Patent and Trademark Office lacks the staff and resources to adequately implement and enforce patent and trademark laws.

These weaknesses in Mexican patent law, along with similar problems regarding trademarks, and to a lesser extent copyrights, caused the U.S. Trade Representative to place Mexico on its priority watch list for intellectual property violations when it implemented Section 182 of the Omnibus Trade and Competitiveness Act of 1988.

Labor Policy. Like many Latin American countries, Mexican statutes seek to aggressively regulate, with widely varying degrees of success, the contract between employers and employees. Matters that might otherwise be left to direct employer-employee negotiations, or collective bargaining in a unionized environment, are specified by law. For example, employers are required to provide a specific number of vacation days, holiday bonuses,[16] severance pay,[17] and profit sharing. Workers are protected by very strong (much stronger than in the United States) wrongful dismissal laws—employers must notify the Labor Ministry when they fire a worker and can be required to show cause.

In Mexico's traditional industrial sector (i.e., excluding the Maquiladoras), workers are highly unionized and the right to bargain collectively has been generally well protected. Firms are required to contribute substantially to funds administered by company-union-government councils that provide subsidized housing, medical care, education grants, savings programs, subsidized loans, and legal services.

Before the crisis of the early 1980s, the average manufacturing wage in Mexico was in the range of 30 percent of U.S. levels; coupled with the above listed benefits, this made urban industrial workers in Mexico fairly well off by developing country standards. In the 1980s, the devaluation of the peso and inflation eroded real wages substantially, while the Maquiladoras, as opposed to the traditional industrial sector, profited from liberalization and the export boom.

With respect to occupational health and safety and child labor regulations, Mexican law provides substantial protection. As with environmental regulations, though, enforcement is uneven.[18] With too few inspectors and other resources, enforcement is generally better in urban areas of the traditional industrial sector. Lax enforcement has been a particular problem in the Maquiladoras where virtually all of the new export competitive production has been created.

In the Maquiladoras, only workers in the state of Tamaulipas on the Gulf Coast are heavily unionized, employees are predominantly young women, and turnover frequently exceeds 100 percent a year. U.S. government officials with considerable experience in Mexico and with its labor movement interviewed for this study indicated that the Mexican government and the Confederation of Mexican Workers (CTM) have not been eager to see the Maquiladoras organized.[19] Traditional Mexican approaches for ensuring adequate living conditions and a safe and reasonably comfortable working environment do not always function effectively in such a nonunion environment.

In testimony before the International Trade Commission (ITC), "a number of U.S. industry representatives, particularly those with Maquiladora operations, insisted that they treat their workers well, providing them with meals, transportation, health care, child care, and a clean working environment, at least compatible with U.S. standards."[20]

However, reports in newspapers such as *The Wall Street Journal* indicate that such claims are not universally true. For example, the paper reports abysmal living conditions—communities lacking sewage and potable water and living in fear of epidemic—around major cities such as Nogales and Tijuana. The blight and acute health risks often spill over into the United States.[21] With regard to working conditions, the *Journal* concludes:

> Many of the maquilas offer clean and relatively pleasant working conditions, and those who toil in them also get some benefits.
>
> Some maquilas resemble sweatshops more than factories. They lack ventilation, and workers may pass out from the heat and fumes. Production demands can put them at risk; Edwviges Ramos Hernandez, a teacher in Juarez, worked at one factory where in a year three workers had fingers sliced off. The machines, she said, were set at a maddening pace.[22]

It is difficult to generalize about living and working conditions across the entire Maquiladora region. However, reports such as these indicate that without a change in federal government and CTM policies, conditions that would be considered absolutely unacceptable in the United States will continue to be commonplace in some Maquiladoras.

Economic Reform in Mexico

Most of Mexico's current difficulties can be traced to the structural legacies of interventionist policies (e.g., inefficient manufacturing and transportation sectors, corruption and an absence of domestic and foreign investor confidence) and to the heavy borrowing that followed the rise in petroleum prices in the early 1970s.[23]

Like many countries flush with new oil wealth, Mexico used the money it borrowed to support an overvalued currency, to maintain higher levels of consumption than it could afford, to purchase foreign assets, and to subsidize inefficient state enterprises. Oil wealth emboldened statist bureaucrats to extend the reach of government and adopt a more independent (hostile) posture toward foreign investment, intellectual property rights and trade.

For example, the 1973 LFI tightened restrictions on foreign investment and the 1976 LIT stripped pharmaceuticals and other products of patent protection. The share of imports controlled by licenses rose from 65 percent in 1969 to 100 percent in 1982. Subsidies to domestic industries (in particular, inefficient parastatals) accounted for some 61 percent of government spending in 1975, as Mexico's fiscal deficit jumped from 2.2 percent in 1969 to 10 percent in 1975. In 1982, the year of Mexico's first debt crisis, it had reached 17.2 percent, as total foreign debt had swollen to $86 billion or 34 percent of Mexico's export revenue. Although the International Monetary Fund (IMF) stepped in with a major loan on the condition that Mexico accept fiscal reforms, spending soon picked up again and the process of economic reform—both macro and micro—did not begin in earnest until after the 1985 earthquake and 1986 oil price slide.

As part of a dramatic turnaround in policy, the federal fiscal deficit fell from 16 percent in 1987 to less than 4.5 percent in 1990. In addition to reining in spending, the new economic policy includes reductions in tariffs and other restrictions on trade, deregulation of the domestic economy, liberalization of foreign investment rules, and divestiture of state enterprises.

Trade Liberalization. In mid-1985, Mexico began liberalizing its trade regime. In 1986, Mexico joined the GATT and subsequently signed the Tokyo Round codes regarding import licensing, dumping, customs valuation, and standards and technical barriers to trade.[24] It has been in the process of bringing many of its policies and practices into conformity with these agreements. At the beginning of 1991, tariffs averaged only about 10 percent, import licenses were required for about 5 percent of customs categories,[25] and reference prices were no longer used to assign customs values to imports.

Mexico joined the GATT as a developing country, and its protocol of accession recognizes the priority status it accords to agriculture in achieving its social and economic development objectives. Most remaining import licenses are concentrated in this sector.

Mexico obtained other concessions in its accession protocol. The restrictions placed on the use of energy and other natural resources by the 1917 Constitution are acknowledged, and Mexico maintains the right to temporarily exclude automobiles, pharmaceuticals and electronics from import license removal timetables. These sectors comprise about one-fourth of the country's manufacturing. They are the focus of industrial development plans that place specific import-substitution and other performance requirements on domestic and foreign firms (discussed below).

Other specific products subjected to import barriers of various kinds include grains and other agricultural commodities, secondary petrochemicals, apparel, home appliances, and other consumer goods.

On a functional level, barriers to imports continue to be posed by government procurement practices, product standards and testing, and domestic working requirements for patents and the complete absence of patent protection for some products.

On the export side, Mexico has phased out most direct subsidies.

Deregulation. The Mexican Secretariat of Commerce and Industrial Development has been given a mandate to deregulate the economy. Among the sectors in which regulations have been or are in the process of being reformed are trucking, multimodal transportation, packaging, finance, insurance, fishing, certain commodities (sugar, cocoa and coffee), agriculture and food processing, petroleum refining, petrochemicals, automotive production, electronics, pharmaceuticals, and the transfer of technology.

New Rules for Foreign Investment. Beginning in 1984, the need for foreign capital prompted a succession of reforms regarding direct investment. Through 1988, many projects with 100 percent foreign ownership were approved, including projects in electrical and nonelectrical machinery and equipment, computers, transportation equipment, chemicals, high-technology services, and hotel sectors. In 1986, the Petroleum Development Plan reclassified 36 petrochemicals from the basic category, where production is reserved for Pemex, to the secondary category, where foreign participation is permitted up to 40 percent. In August 1989, another 35 basic petrochemicals were reclassified to secondary, leaving only 20 products on the basic list. These and other reforms were achieved through presidential decree, as opposed to changes in the 1973 LFI.

In May 1989, a new decree, Regulations of the Law to Promote Mexican Investment and Regulate Foreign Investment, made sweeping changes in the investment regime. Essentially, those categories in which ownership is reserved to the state or to Mexican nationals or in which foreign participation is limited to 34 or 40 percent remain intact (items a, b and c listed on page 22). However, for remaining activities, the 49 percent foreign ownership restriction applies to a limited number of industries; where 100 percent foreign ownership is now permitted, not all investors are required to seek CNIE approval.

    d. Activities subject to the 49 percent limitation—fisheries; mining other than uranium, coal, iron ore, phosphoric rock and sulfur; extraction of rocks, clays and sand—e.g., gypsum and spar; manufacture of explosives and fireworks; manufacture and specialized trade in firearms; internal port, river and lake transportation services; telecommunications services, except telegraphs; and rental agencies.

    e. Activities in which CNIE authorization is required for up to 100 percent foreign ownership—livestock and game; newspapers and magazines; derivatives of carbon minerals (coke); construction; maritime transportation on the high seas; tourist boat rental services; administration of passenger bus stations, roads, bridges, and auxiliary services; air navigation services and administration of airports and heliports; vehicle towing services; educational services provided by private vendors; legal, accounting and auditing services; and insurance and financial services not otherwise restricted.

New foreign investments in "unclassified sectors" are automatically approved if they entail investments of less than $100 million; are funded with resources from abroad; are located outside of Mexico City, Guadalajara and Monterrey; are anticipated to create balanced foreign exchange flows over the first three years; will increase employment and establish worker training and personnel development programs; and utilize adequate technologies to environmental requirements. Stock purchases in unclassified sectors that raise foreign investors' holdings above 49 percent require CNIE approval. New Maquiladora investments and similar export-oriented activities do not require CNIE authorization.

The expansion of existing investment through new projects, activities or product lines does not require CNIE approval if it involves a Maquiladora, other export-oriented activity, results from a merger, or the owner agrees to increase investment by 10

percent of the net asset value and the criteria for unclassified investments noted above are met.

For all other investments, CNIE approval continues to be required but the review process has been streamlined, simplified and made more transparent; reviews must be completed within 45 days of application or approval becomes automatic. In sectors reserved for Mexican nationals or in which foreign ownership is limited to 34, 40 or 49 percent, foreign participation may be increased through 20-year investment trusts authorized by the CNIE, under certain circumstances.[26] Also, Mexican nationals may establish neutral investment trusts in these sectors.

Application processes to establish real estate investment trusts through Mexican banks have been similarly streamlined; these 30-year trusts are now automatically renewable under their original terms and conditions.[27]

In 1990, the Mexican government began permitting foreigners to purchase nonvoting, minority positions (up to 49 percent) in insurance and reinsurance companies. It also announced it would permit foreigners to purchase up to 30 percent of state-owned commercial banks, with individual investments limited to 10 percent, nonvoting positions. In 1991, the Mexican government began divesting the commercial banks nationalized in 1982 and is now permitting 30 percent foreign ownership, with individual positions limited to 10 percent voting.

These reforms constitute a major improvement in the environment for foreign investors in Mexico. However, Mexico is still imposing significant performance requirements. These are oriented toward creating employment and exports and can significantly affect production and employment in the United States.

Privatization. Privatization of government enterprises, and eliminating the subsidies they receive, has been a key element in Mexican economic liberalization. About three-fourths of the approximately 1,200 parastatals have been sold, merged or closed. These efforts include the sale of the national telephone company (Telemex) and two national airlines (Aeromexico and Compania Mexicana de Aviacon). The government has reduced its holdings in food processing, soft drinks, fishing, automotive products (including Renault de Mexico), textiles, chemicals (including petrochemicals), wood and paper products, and other construction materials. The Salinas Administration has indicated that it wishes to sell off all parastatals except Pemex and CFE (the national electricity company).

Intellectual Property. In January 1990, the Mexican government unveiled draft legislation that would strengthen intellectual property laws by lengthening patent protection to 20 years, increasing the range of products and processes receiving patent protection (including pharmaceuticals and many others for which patent coverage had been postponed until 1997), significantly limiting the practice of compulsory licensing, enhancing and increasing the term of trademark protection, and strengthening the capacity of the Mexican Patent and Trademark Office to process and enforce intellectual property laws.

Sectoral Policies

In addition to these changes in general economic policy, Mexico has made many revisions in development strategies for priority sectors—computers, pharmaceuticals and automobiles. Overall, the changes complement the process of liberalization, although these policies are still fairly aggressive by the standards of advanced industrialized countries.

Computer Industry. Prior to 1981, Mexico imported virtually all its computer equipment. In that year, foreign companies were required to establish domestic production facilities and were subjected to tough performance requirements to maintain access to the Mexican market. Firms wishing to import into Mexico were required to negotiate specific production, import-substitution, local content, R&D, and exporting goals.

To encourage production, firms were offered tax incentives; preferential treatment in government procurement, energy pricing and financing; and protection from imports. Performance requirements were negotiated on a firm by firm basis. This process led to many foreign companies being exempt from the 49 percent ceiling on foreign ownership—most Mexican computer manufacturers are 100 percent foreign owned.

As part of the overall liberalization process, import licenses for all computer products were eliminated in April 1990, and tariffs were raised to 20 percent for final computer products, 10 percent for parts and components and 5 percent on some scarce inputs.[28] However, restrictions continue on imports of used computers and on the employment of U.S. maintenance, repair and consulting personnel.

Pharmaceutical Industry. The government of Mexico has employed a variety of techniques to encourage domestic manufacturing of pharmaceuticals. In 1976, the LIT stripped drugs of patent protection in Mexico. In 1985, the government pursued a policy of requiring drug manufacturers to list generic ingredients on their labels, and it established strict price controls. In addition, the government offered firms a fixed period of protection (e.g., five years) from imports establishing production of specific drugs. By 1988, 88 such agreements were in place, but the government is permitting these to lapse as their terms expire. The government also offers procurement preferences to drug producers; however, the major remaining impediment to U.S. drug exports is the absence of patent protection, and this should be largely corrected by the recently proposed legislation discussed above.

Automobile Industry. Motor vehicle production in Mexico is dominated by foreign MNCs, with General Motors, Chrysler and Ford assembling 60 percent of all cars and German and Japanese automakers accounting for the balance. The parts industry, composed of about 100 companies, has traditionally focused on low-technology items, but this is changing as U.S. firms increase their investments. Each year, Mexico exports about half of its 400 to 500 million vehicle production. In addition, it exports up to 1.2 million engines to the United States, Europe and Japan.

Since 1962, the Mexican government has imposed rigid production, domestic sourcing and export performance requirements on manufacturers to encourage the development of the domestic industry and foster a favorable trade balance. The 1983 Automotive Decree limited the number of lines and models that vehicle manufacturers could produce and required that local content for each type of vehicle increase each year from 1984 to 1987. With respect to the latter, the goals for automobiles, light trucks and medium trucks were 60, 70 and 80 percent, respectively. Similarly, autoparts manufacturers were required to raise local content to 60 percent. Imports of vehicles were effectively prohibited. Companies were required to earn, through exports, the foreign exchange necessary to cover their imports and to meet 50 percent of this requirement through parts sales. Overall, the emphasis was on developing the parts industry.[29]

The 1989 decree substantially liberalized these regulations. Vehicle producers are no longer restricted in the number of lines and models they may produce. The decree established an overall (labor and parts) 36 percent content requirement for vehicles and 30 percent for parts. Companies are now able to specialize by importing some vehicles and exporting others; however, the ratio of the value of imports to exports must exceed 2.5 to 1 in 1991, declining in stages to 1.75 to 1 in 1994. Imports of cars with engines under 1.8 liters are banned until the 1993 model year. The government has indicated that it plans to phase out import restrictions but has not set a deadline for such action.

CONCLUDING REMARKS

Since the mid-1980s, Mexico City has achieved remarkable progress in opening up its economy to international competition, increasing the role of private decisions in economic management and removing barriers to the efficient allocation of resources. However, substantial aspects of the old regime remain and await additional reforms. How the process plays out with regard to further deregulation, privatization and liberalization of foreign investment and intellectual property regimes will strongly affect whether the proposed free trade agreement benefits the United States and Canada. These general policies, as well as Mexico's sectoral strategies, could be crafted in ways that promote a level playing field or they could disadvantage U.S. and Canadian firms and workers. For example, continuation of foreign investment performance requirements or export/import goals in the automotive sector would disadvantage U.S. and Canadian workers in the competition for jobs.

Along the same lines, inadequate enforcement of environmental and workplace safety standards lower costs for producers seeking to avoid reasonable regulations and standards of safe practice in the United States and Canada. Again, this disadvantages American and Canadian workers.

Overall, a free trade agreement that does not address these issues, either directly or through parallel processes, can disadvantage the United States and Canada. In contrast, an agreement that provides meaningful arrangements can offer Americans and Canadians opportunities to address their legitimate concerns about the effects of Mexican policies and practices on competition in the North American marketplace.

NOTES

1. Consider, for example, the differences between the United States and the EC regarding agricultural subsidies, the difficulties the United States has had in collecting on Japanese commitments in their bilateral talks, and the continued use of orderly marketing agreements and grey area measures to manage EC, U.S. and Canadian trade with Japan and the NICs.

2. See Peter Morici, "The Environment for Free Trade," "The Implications for U.S. Policy" and "Living with Free Trade" in *Making Free Trade Work: The Canada-U.S. Agreement* (New York: Council on Foreign Relations), pp. 10–12, 129–131 and 166–167.

3. The term Rector is used by Mexicans to refer to the government's role as guardian, for example, to ensure fairness for all participants in the economy, to safeguard against foreign domination, and to promote socially desirable patterns of economic development.

4. The federally sponsored National Assessment of Educational Progress indicates that only 5 to 8 percent of all 17-year olds demonstrates the skills needed to function in demanding jobs or to do college work as traditionally defined. See Educational Testing Service, *America's Challenge: Accelerating Academic Achievement* (Princeton, 1990).

These findings are supplemented by a large, growing body of evidence that U.S. high school graduates have received educations that are inferior (by several grade levels) to their peers' educations abroad. See, for example, John Bishop, "Incentives for Learning: Why American High School Students Compare Poorly to Their Counterparts Overseas," Center for Advance Human Resources Studies Working Paper 89-09 (Ithaca: Cornell University, 1989).

5. See Commission on the Skills of the American Workforce, *America's Choice: high skills or low wages!* (Rochester, New York: National Center on Education and the Economy, 1990), p. 24.

6. This is one reason why, for example, Japanese automakers are better able to pursue their product development and capital expansion plans for the North American market at a time of sluggish sales than Ford, even though the latter has made enormous leaps in productivity, quality and product design in recent years.

7. This section on Mexican economy, reforms and sectoral policies draws substantially from the following sources: USITC, *Review of Trade and Investment Liberalization Measures by Mexico and Prospects for Future United States-Mexican Relations*, USITC Report No. 2275 (April 1990) and No. 2326 (October 1990); USITC, *The Likely Impact on the United States of a Free Trade Agreement with Mexico*, USITC Report No. 2353 (February 1991); U.S. Embassy in Mexico City, *Economic Trends Report* (December 1990) and *Foreign Investment Climate Statement* (August 1990); Committee for the Promotion of Investment in Mexico, *Mexico and the Foreign Investor* (Mexico City, May 1989); and discussions with U.S., Mexican and Canadian government officials and academics and U.S. labor officials.

Additional information was obtained from Sidney Weintraub, *Transforming the Mexican Economy: The Salinas Sexenio* (Washington: National Planning Association, 1990); U.S. Embassy in Mexico City, *Petroleum Report* (July 1990); Committee for the Promotion of Investment in Mexico, *Mexico: Economic and Business Overview* (Mexico City, June 1990) and *The Competitiveness of the Mexican Economy* (Mexico City, 1990); Government of Mexico, Office of the President, *Toward a Mexico-U.S. Free Trade Agreement* (1990); Government of Mexico, *The Mexican Agenda* (October 1990); Department of State, *Country Reports on Human Rights Practices for 1990, Report Submitted to the Committee on Foreign Relations, U.S. Senate and the Committee on Foreign Affairs House of Representatives* (February 1990); Robert S. Gay, *Mexico on the Mend* (New York: Morgan Stanley, 1991); Wilson Peres Nunez, *From Globalization to Regionalization: The Mexican Case* (Paris: OECD, 1990); John F.H. Purcell and Dirk W. Damrau, *Mexico: A World Class Economy* (New York: Solomon Brothers, 1990); Economist Intelligence Unit, *Mexico Country Report* (London: 1990); General Accounting Office, *U.S.-Mexico Trade: Trends and Impediments in Agricultural Trade* (June 1990); Peat Marwick Policy Economics Group, *The Effects of a Free Trade Agreement Between the U.S. and Mexico* (New York, 1991); Office of the U.S. Trade Representative, *National Trade*

Estimates Report on Foreign Trade Barriers (1986, 1987, 1989, and 1990); *Business International* (various issues); *Latin American International* (various issues); *Bureau of National Affairs International Trade Reporter* (various issues); *Mexico Business New Summary* (various issues); and *Survey of Current Business* (various issues).

8. For example, see Raul Prebisch, "Commercial Policies in the Underdeveloped Countries," *American Economic Review* (May 1959), pp. 251–273.

9. It also should be recognized that during this period, governments in many Western countries, such as Canada and Europe, chose to own suppliers of essential services like electricity and telecommunications rather than grant limited monopolies and regulate them as was the practice in the United States.

10. Pemex, the national petroleum monopoly, accounted for about two-fifths of this.

11. Until 1986, Mexico was not a member of the GATT; therefore, it was not subject to its disciplines regarding its trade practices.

12. Foreigners investing, for example, in resorts or Maquiladoras may obtain virtually all the property rights to land in the restricted zone by purchasing land through a bank trustee. The bank holds the bare title, and the foreign investor may improve the land or transfer the title. Such trusts are limited to 30 years.

13. Foreign ownership in certain strategic minerals was limited to 34 percent.

14. In 1982, all commercial banks, except Citibank and one domestic bank, were nationalized. Citibank may not open new offices or become a multiple service bank.

15. The range of activities in which the government has sold assets since 1985 bears the strongest witness to this—discussed below in this section.

16. Employers must provide a 25 percent bonus during vacation periods and a Christmas bonus equal to 15 days pay.

17. Three months wages plus 20 days pay per year worked up to 12 years. Workers employed over 12 years are entitled to an additional 12 days pay per year worked.

18. Mexican environmental regulations and enforcement are discussed in Chapter 3.

19. As has been the case with environmental enforcement, Mexico City has been careful not to discourage American investors.

20. USITC Report No. 2326, p. 1–12.

21. For example, San Elixario, Texas, shares a contaminated aquifer with Mexico. By the time that children in this area have reached the age of 8, 35 percent of them have had hepatitis, and 90 percent of the adult population by age 35 has had the disease, too.

22. Sonia Nazario, "Boom and Despair," *The Wall Street Journal* (September 22, 1989), R26.

23. For a concise review of the forces giving rise to economic reform in Mexico, the reader is refered to Weintraub, *Transforming the Mexican Economy*.

24. Mexico has not yet signed the Subsidies or Procurement Codes, although it has a 1985 understanding with the United States regarding the use of subsidies and countervailing duties.

25. These categories still accounted for about 25 percent of Mexican trade by value.

26. Approval is far from automatic. A trust will be approved if it is needed to improve the financial or operating condition of firms in a classified sector, the foreign investment is in the form of cash or capitalization of company liabilities, and Mexican investors have been offered right of first refusal. These trusts must provide for sale of shares to the Mexican public after 20 years.

27. See footnote number 12.

28. Companies with production facilities in Mexico are eligible for tariff reductions for a three-year period. The size of these benefits depends on their level of domestic production, local content and Mexican R&D.

29. This stands in contrast to the policy of encouraging vehicle production in Canada through its 1965 Automotive Agreement with the United States.

Commercial Relations with Mexico

3

This chapter provides some additional background on the current trade negotiations. Mexico's trade and industrial policies inhibit U.S. and Canadian sales in Mexico and in many areas increase Mexican sales in the United States and Canada. The current effort to negotiate a new North American regime is best seen in the context of these policies, of the bilateral trade agreements negotiated in recent years to limit the effects of these policies on U.S./Canadian-Mexican trade, and of the overall patterns of trade that have emerged from the combined effects of government policies and comparative advantages. The first two parts of this chapter describe the trade agreements already in place and the policies and practices affecting trade that should be important in negotiations with Mexico. The chapter concludes with a brief review of the patterns of U.S. and Canadian trade with Mexico, which provides some indication of the nature of adjustments that would be imposed by a free trade agreement.

TRADE AGREEMENTS WITH MEXICO

The basic agreement governing commercial relations between the United States and Canada, on the one hand, and Mexico, on the other hand, is the GATT, which is supplemented by several bilateral accords. The latter are particularly important in areas such as subsidies where Mexico is not a signatory of the GATT code; in areas such as intellectual property where GATT coverage is limited; and in sectoral policies where Mexico has engaged in practices outside GATT norms[1] owing to its developing country status and the terms of its GATT accession.[2] Overall, the United States has found it necessary to go beyond the GATT in trade relations with Mexico because of the volume of their bilateral trade and the aggressive nature of Mexican policies that are not adequately or easily addressed through the GATT. In many ways, the proposed free trade agreement would continue that process if U.S. interests on a wide enough range of issues were addressed.

GATT

The liberalization measures discussed in Chapter 2 go a long way toward bringing Mexico's trade regime and the management of its domestic economy into conformity with GATT norms.

As Mexico sheds its state-managed approach to economic development and becomes more open to foreign competition, its industries become more vulnerable to the kinds of unfair competition that emanate from the policies Mexico pursued with such vigor in the past. Shortly before joining the GATT, Mexico made major changes in its trade laws, establishing subsidy/countervailing duty and antidumping laws similar to those applied by the United States and Canada.[3]

Notably in the context of bilateral and trilateral negotiations, Mexico applies a weaker injury test in subsidy and dumping cases than required by the GATT. This attracted some attention from GATT members at the time of Mexican accession. Also, when Mexico signed the GATT dumping code, unlike most other GATT members, it gave the code treaty status. This gives the code equal standing with domestic law in the Mexican legal system[4] and sets an interesting precedent for future U.S./Canada-Mexico agreements regarding politically sensitive issues such as investment.

Understanding on Subsidies and Countervailing Duties (1985)

In 1985, the United States and Mexico signed an Understanding on Subsidies and Countervailing Duties. Essentially, the United States agreed to apply an injury test in subsidy/countervailing duty investigations. Mexico agreed (1) to eliminate certain of its then active tax rebate programs for exports and the subsidy elements of its export financing programs; and (2) to phase out energy and basic petrochemical pricing practices that had the purpose or effect of subsidizing exports.[5]

It is important to understand fully the scope and limitations of the second commitment. In 1985, Pemex sold to all domestic customers natural gas and certain petroleum products used in energy-intensive industries at prices below international levels; further, Pemex had special programs that provided energy and feedstocks at costs below prevailing domestic prices to the petrochemical and other industries. This essentially established a three-tier pricing system—export, domestic and special use. As per the 1985 agreement, Mexico phased out special use prices (turning a three-tier pricing system into a two-tier system), while it continued to price natural gas and certain other petroleum products below international levels.[6] Mexican officials argued that the latter practice was justified and reflected its comparative advantage. The resulting benefits are generally available to all domestic consumers and industrial users; therefore, this practice has been found not to provide a countervailable subsidy under U.S. statute.[7] More important, though, this episode establishes the precedent that Mexico does not view international agreements regarding its internal energy pricing as prohibited by the 1917 Constitution.

United States-Mexico Framework Understanding (1987)

The agreement established the first formal framework for management of bilateral commercial relations. It established a mechanism for the two countries to consult on trade issues, resolve disputes and reduce trade barriers. In addition, it initiated discussions in a number of contentious areas,[8] and these contributed to progress in areas such as electronics, investment and intellectual property, and in sectoral agreements increasing Mexican access to the U.S. market for apparel and steel and increasing U.S. access to the Mexican market for alcoholic beverages.

Also as an outgrowth of the framework agreement, the two countries signed a U.S.-Mexican Standards Agreement in 1988. They agreed to establish common health and safety standards regarding crossborder commerce in food, drugs, cosmetics, medical equipment, and other biologicals.

Understanding Regarding Trade and Investment Facilitation Talks (1989)

This agreement goes beyond the 1987 framework understanding, which focused on disputes and mandated discussions on a number of specific sectoral and functional areas. The Trade and Investment Facilitation Talks (TIFTs) mandate a comprehensive negotiation process and joint study groups to provide facts and data for this process. The initial topics were product standards and testing and petrochemicals. However, the TIFTs have been overtaken by efforts to prepare for the bilateral free trade negotiations. As part of the latter process, bilateral working groups were established in December 1990 to focus on agriculture, automotive trade, financial services, insurance, petrochemicals, rules of origin, tariffs, technical barriers to trade (standards), and land transport.

Canadian Agreements with Mexico

Until Mexico joined the GATT, the principal agreements governing trade between Canada and Mexico were their Trade

Agreement of 1946 and an Agreement on Industrial and Energy Cooperation of 1980. On the occasion of President Mulroney's visit to Mexico in March 1990, the two countries entered into an Agreement on a Trade and Investment Consultation System, which is similar to the U.S.-Mexican framework agreement.[9]

BARRIERS TO TRADE AND INVESTMENT

U.S. and Canadian Trade Barriers

U.S. and Canadian tariffs on Mexican imports average about 3.5 and 2.4 on an import weighted basis. These averages can be deceptive because Mexican exports tend to be concentrated in areas where tariffs are low or nonexistent[10] and do not take into account the trade discouraged in sectors where some or many tariffs remain high.

In agriculture, the United States applies seasonal tariffs, which can be as high as 25 percent, on some Mexican fruit and vegetables. U.S. marketing orders—which set grade, quality and size standards—on products such as tomatoes, onions, avocadoes, grapefruit, oranges, olives, and table grapes are perceived by Mexican growers as barriers to market access. To defend domestic price supports, the United States maintains quotas on meat and dairy products, sugar and sugar containing products, peanuts and cotton.[11]

Voluntary restraint agreements in apparel and steel limit Mexican exports to the United States. Removing these restrictions would have a much greater impact on Mexican exports to the United States and Canada than eliminating tariffs.

In the automotive sector, the Canada-U.S. FTA applies a strict 50 percent U.S.-Canadian content requirement, potentially limiting the use of Mexican and other foreign components in vehicles assembled in the United States (Canada) destined for the Canadian (U.S.) market.

The threat that access to the U.S. market may be closed by safeguard actions, subsidy/countervailing and antidumping duties or the application of other trade remedy laws is, perhaps, the most important Mexican concern in the current negotiations.[12] Obtaining security of access through a dispute settlement process similar to one embodied in the FTA should be a key Mexican objective in these talks.

Inconsistent and cumbersome U.S. customs procedures have been cited as problematic by business executives and officials on both sides of the border. As the International Trade

Commission concluded in a recent survey of views regarding bilateral liberalization:

> The most egregious barrier cited by participants was the U.S. Customs procedures at the border. Mexican exporters, U.S. manufacturers of maquila products reentering the United States and several U.S. government officials in Mexico were unanimous in decrying procedural impediments to trade, including "inefficient and capricious" import regulations. . . . [13]

In addition, as the process of integrating Mexico into the U.S. and Canadian economies continues, some U.S. and Canadian practices that were issues in the FTA negotiations will come to the foreground. In Canada, these include federal and provincial procurement practices (such as Canadian Treasury Board guidelines encouraging domestic sourcing), foreign investment performance requirements (the FTA exempts the United States from many of these but does not exempt third countries), and the various subsidies and other benefits offered through federal and provincial industrial policies. In the United States, these include federal and state procurement preferences (e.g., the requirements of the Surface Transportation Act of 1978 and the Public Works Act of 1977) and various state industrial incentives. [14]

Mexico: Traditional Trade Issues

As discussed, Mexico has substantially liberalized its import regime. As of early 1991, the maximum tariff was 20 percent and tariffs averaged about 10 percent. Generally, rates rise with the amount of processing products receive. For example, in the agricultural sector, tariffs on bulk commodities are generally low, while duties for processed foods and alcoholic beverages are high. [15] Among the products facing the highest tariffs are automotive products, secondary petrochemicals, telecommunications equipment, glass products, fish, canned fruit and vegetables, coffee and other beverages, tobacco products, apparel, detergents, cosmetics, home appliances, and other consumer goods. [16]

In recent years, most import permit requirements have been concentrated in strategic and priority sectors identified by the Mexican government for development assistance and in agriculture. The former includes policies in automotive products and pharmaceuticals discussed above. Regarding agriculture, about 40 percent of U.S. farm exports to Mexico were affected by licenses in 1991—controlled products included grains, oilseeds, dairy products, and certain horticultural products. According to U.S. Trade Representative Carla Hills, these licenses are often granted and withheld in an arbitrary fashion. [17]

Mexican product standards and testing requirements also pose problems. For example, Mexico does not accept foreign test data for telecommunications equipment, and U.S. industry officials complain about the arbitrary application of health regulations for breeding cattle.[18]

As in the United States and Canada, Mexican government agencies display a pronounced preference for domestic goods. Such preferences severely limit, for example, U.S. sales of construction and engineering services in airport, highway, port, and tourism facilities.[19] As important, this preference extends to parastatal enterprises—for example, as they have affected purchases of telecommunications equipment (i.e., Telmex and Telcomm) and steel.[20] Although many of these firms are being privatized, old habits may prove difficult to break.

In other areas, Mexican customs practices, such as surcharges and excessive processing fees that raise nominal tariffs, the inadequate protection of patents and trademarks, and foreign investment screening and performance requirements limit the penetration of U.S. and Canadian products into Mexican markets.

The effects of these practices are exacerbated by inadequacies in the Mexican customs service and transportation and communications infrastructures. As the ITC reported in its recent survey of views:

> Several witnesses . . . testified that the inadequacies of existing customs facilities result in congestion and considerable delays on the border. Participants suggested that access into Mexico could be improved by upgrading both countries' facilities, notably their computer systems, and by coordinating customs' computer facilities with those of the railroads.[21]

In the service sector, restrictions on foreign ownership of commercial banks, insurance and reinsurance companies, securities firms, and other financial service firms pose very considerable barriers to foreign participation in activities in which both the United States and Canada enjoy comparative advantages.

Mexico: Environmental and Workplace Issues

To these practices must be added other aspects of Mexican policy that may offer an unfair advantage to production in Mexico over production in the United States and Canada. Issues such as environmental enforcement and workplace health and safety standards are not headline issues in multilateral trade talks because they would be very costly to deal with in that process.

However, when large contiguous economies become engaged in efforts to create an integrated economy, these subjects become important.

As trade liberalization extends to virtually full market integration—as the United States and Canada envision under the FTA and could be the outcome of talks with Mexico—the potential for distortions of business decisions rises asymptotically with the scope of integration. As the ITC observed in its recent report on EC 1992:

> The "social dimension" of EC 92 refers to the efforts to harmonize different EC member-state policies on labor markets, industrial relations systems, occupational safety and health regulations, social welfare, and social security. Although the White Paper did not call for legislative action in this area, as integration progressed, it was recognized that *some harmonization of working conditions was necessary to avoid distortion in labor markets and prevent abuses of competition.*[22]

Also, with the passage of the Single European Act of 1987, the Community was given for the first time explicit authority to enforce member-state implementation of its environmental legislation.

In the Canada-U.S. FTA talks, environmental and workplace safety issues did not come up because the United States and Canada already have comparable laws and are engaged in continuous processes to resolve transborder problems.[23] Generally, differences between U.S. and Canadian standards and enforcement are not large enough to affect profoundly bilateral patterns of trade and specialization. However, with regard to Mexico, lower standards and lax enforcement have been problems in some areas.

In March 1988, Mexico enacted a comprehensive environmental protection law, the Ecologic Equilibrium and Environmental Protection Act, and SEDUE (Mexico's equivalent of the EPA) has issued regulations regarding the reporting and disposal of toxic wastes. Mexico is making some effort to enforce these laws—for example, SEDUE has begun temporarily closing Maquiladora plants for environmental infractions.[24] However, as in any developing country, resources for enforcement are scarce, and environmental groups cite numerous problems.[25] In the words of one SEDUE official: "Carrying out the law requires lots of people who are well trained. It requires lots of laboratory equipment. You must remember, we are not a developed nation. We are of the Third World."[26]

Moreover, Mexican officials are cautious not to discourage

Maquiladora investment. According to the *Los Angeles Times:* "Although the nation is tightening up enforcement of a sweeping set of industrial pollution standards passed in 1988, several Mexican officials stressed in interviews that they are taking a flexible approach to pollution issues relating to Maquiladoras."[27]

Also, Mexican standards are significantly lower than U.S. state standards in some areas. For example, California has adopted tough and costly rules regarding the use of ozone-creating, solvent-based paints, stains and lacquers. This gives other U.S. states and Mexico a decided cost advantage; however, with other states likely to follow California's lead, furniture manufacturers have no choice but to flock to Mexico—if they do not, their competitors will.

Overall, lax enforcement and lower standards attract firms from the United States seeking to avoid environmental costs and place competitive pressures on other firms, who might otherwise wish to be more responsible, to join them. In this way, lax environmental enforcement has effects much like those of subsidies—it attracts production and jobs, distorts trade and creates unemployment in responsible jurisdictions.

Lax environmental enforcement, like subsidies and many other domestic policies that affect the location of production and employment, are very difficult to address effectively in multilateral trade talks. However, in regional talks aimed at creating a free trade area, environmental harmonization is a more tractable task, and the potential trade distorting consequences of lax enforcement are much greater than they are in the context of GATT negotiations. Hence, the logic for including environmental issues, either directly or through parallel discussions, in trade negotiations with Mexico is strong.

Similarly, lax enforcement of Mexican workplace and health and safety standards, discussed in Chapter 2, can have similar effects. Running a sweatshop is not attractive to most employers. However, when the opportunities created by lax enforcement attract some firms to the Maquiladora zone, competitors in the United States and elsewhere in Mexico are penalized for offering decent and humane working conditions—they are placed at a decided competitive disadvantage.

Academics can argue that lower Mexican wages reflect Mexican comparative advantages; this is a tough reality we have to accept in the United States and Canada. However, unsafe working conditions of the kind described in Chapter 2 are not a reality we have to accept in a free trade partner. Should the United States, Canada and Mexico move toward full free trade, so that firms and workers in northern Mexico compete with firms and workers in

New York and Montreal on the same basis as their counterparts in California, the enforcement of workplace health and safety standards in Tijuana and Nogales becomes as valid an economic concern for apparel workers in New York and Montreal as is the enforcement of OHSA rules in California.

Academic economists and many industry advocates of free trade argue that a trade pact with Mexico would permit a favorable exchange of jobs. However, such an exchange would truly reflect comparative advantages only if meaningful workplace health and safety standards were enforced in Mexico. The cost savings associated with poor working conditions and lax enforcement have already proved too strong an attraction for some U.S. employers, and they place American workers at an unfair disadvantage. As discussed in Chapter 6, effective enforcement of meaningful workplace standards should be a key issue in the upcoming negotiations.

Mexico: The Legacy of a Parastatal Culture

Finally, another set of issues should be recognized— Mexico's revolutionary and parastatal legacy. This may be best appreciated in the context of how free trade agreements relate to the GATT.

Fundamentally, GATT law has been shaped by the American notion that the structure of international trade and specialization should be driven by market signals—GATT rules seek to encourage member nations to accept and specialize in their areas of comparative advantage. Ensuring such an outcome has increasingly required that GATT rules penetrate domestic policy prerogatives—such as procedures for setting standards and the criteria for offering regional and industrial subsidies. Progress in these areas has become increasingly difficult because, among other reasons, countries vary so much in the degree to which they subscribe to, and how they interpret, the American market paradigm and in their legal and economic institutions. EC 1992 and the FTA became possible because the major participants were already very similar in these aspects and were undergoing considerable processes of convergence after the early 1980s.[28]

While Mexico may be dismantling the bulwarks of statism at a breakneck pace, it will continue to have a revolutionary heritage and its people will continue to look to Mexico City for a Rector. Inevitably, this will affect the character of new economic and legal institutions. In the context of free trade negotiations, the resulting differences in the economic institutions of Mexico and its two partners to the north could make a meeting of the minds on a wide range of nontariff issues cumbersome, even when all parties have the best intentions.

STRUCTURE OF TRADE

A comprehensive North American free trade area would combine the world's largest, eighth-largest and thirteenth-largest economies into a common economic space that would rival the European Community (see Table 2).

Canada is already the United States' largest trading partner, accounting for 22 and 19 percent of U.S. exports and imports, while Mexico is the United States' third largest partner, accounting for 7 and 6 percent of U.S. exports and imports. The United States already accounts for more than 70 percent of Canadian trade and more than 65 percent of Mexican trade, but trade between Canada and Mexico is minimal—less than 2 percent of each country's trade—as their industries compete largely in the U.S. market.

The structure of trade between the United States and Mexico has been influenced as much by the two countries' industrial and trade policies as it has been by comparative advantages. Prior to the liberalization of the mid-1980s, Mexico sought to limit its dependence on U.S. products. U.S. sales in Mexico were domi-

TABLE 2
SIZE OF THE NORTH AMERICAN MARKET*

	GNP ($ Bills.)	Population (Mills.)
United States	4,900	248
Canada	472	26
Mexico	209	85
Total	5,581	359
EC	4,720	365
Japan and Four Asian Tigers	3,202	199

*1989 data or latest available year.

Source: Sidney Weintraub, "Latin American Economic Prospects for the 1990s" (mimeo), (Washington: Center for Strategic and International Studies, December 1990); U.S. Embassy in Mexico City, *Economic Trends Report* (December 1990); and *World Development Report* (Washington: World Bank, 1991).

nated by producer durables and automotive products (49 percent of U.S. exports in 1979). These were supplemented by whatever chemicals (12 percent) and mineral products (7 percent) that Mexico could not provide for itself under its highly autarkic trade regime. Some consumer goods and luxury items came in over high tariffs. Well-to-do Mexicans have a strong preference for U.S. products, much as well-to-do Americans display preferences for certain Japanese and European products. Since the opening of the Mexican market, U.S. sales in all these areas have expanded rapidly (see Table 3).

At the close of the 1970s, Mexico's exports to the United States were dominated by oil. Industries such as apparel, textiles and basic steel, which had been so prominent in the emergence of the East Asian NICs, were encouraged by Mexican industrial policies to be domestically oriented and were inefficient and uncompetitive. The major sectors making use of inexpensive Mexican labor for export to the United States were telecommunications and electrical equipment.

When oil prices collapsed in the early 1980s, Mexico was forced to develop efficient manufacturing industries to service its external debt and to pay for the industrial equipment that would be necessary for modernization. It could not turn to apparel, textiles and basic steel. Although the United States has permitted some additional imports in these areas, Mexico's historically small shares of the U.S. market were locked in by voluntary restraint agreements. The combined contribution of these sectors to Mexican sales in the United States was only about 6 percent. Instead, the biggest areas of growth have been in telecommunications, electrical power generating equipment, other electrical machinery, automotive products, and various other industrial machinery and transportation equipment. In 1989, these sectors accounted for 45 percent of Mexican merchandise exports to the United States.

The Maquiladoras have played an important role in this process, and about one-third of all U.S. direct investments in Mexico are concentrated in these activities. Through this process of trade and investment, Mexico has specialized in low-technology assembly operations, and the United States has specialized in sophisticated components. In some sectors, for example automotive products, Mexican workers are increasingly taking on more sophisticated assignments and, as discussed below, this may significantly raise the adjustment costs imposed by free trade on American workers.

Mexico's trade with Canada underwent a dramatic change in the 1980s. In 1979, Mexico sent mostly food and raw materials

TABLE 3
THE DISTRIBUTION OF U.S. TRADE WITH MEXICO, 1979 AND 1989
(Percent)

SITC		Imports 1979	Imports 1989	Exports 1979	Exports 1989
0	Food and Live Animals	16.6	8.9	8.0	8.3
1	Beverages and Tobacco	0.9	0.9	*	0.1
2	Crude Materials, Inedible except Minerals	3.1	2.5	6.9	6.2
3	Mineral Fuels, Lubricants and Related Products	35.2	16.2	2.4	3.0
32	Coal, Coke and Briquettes	*	*	0.5	0.1
33	Petroleum and Related Products	35.1	15.9	1.2	2.2
34	Gas, Natural and Manufactured	0.1	0.3	0.8	0.7
4	Animal and Vegetable Oils, Fats, Waxes	*	0.1	0.5	0.6
5	Chemicals and Related Products, NES	2.2	2.2	11.5	9.1
51	Organic Chemicals	0.3	0.6	4.8	2.8
52	Inorganic Chemicals	1.4	0.8	1.4	0.9
53	Dyeing, Tanning, Coloring Materials	*	0.1	0.1	0.3
54	Medicinal, Pharmaceutical Products	0.1	0.1	0.4	0.3
55	Essential Oils, Perfumes, Soaps, Cleansers	0.2	0.1	0.4	0.3
56	Fertilizers, Manufactured	*	*	0.4	0.2
57	Explosives, Pyrotechnic Products	*	0.1	*	2.3
58	Artificial Resins and Plastics, Ethers	*	0.2	2.2	1.2
59	Chemical Materials and Products	0.1	0.1	1.6	0.9
6	Manufactured Goods Classified by Mat.	9.9	10.1	13.0	12.3
61	Leather and Furskins	0.2	0.1	0.2	0.1
62	Rubber Manufactures	0.1	0.4	0.7	0.7
63	Cord and Wood Manufactures	1.0	0.4	0.2	0.3
64	Paper, Paperboard, Articles of Pulp	0.6	1.4	1.7	2.6
65	Textile Yarns, Fabrics, NES	0.7	0.7	1.1	1.6
66	Nonmetallic Mineral Manufactures, NES	1.2	1.7	0.9	0.7
67	Iron and Steel	0.8	1.1	4.1	1.9
68	Nonferrous Metals	4.2	2.6	1.6	1.5
69	Manufactures of Metals	1.1	1.7	2.6	2.9
7	Machinery and Transport Equipment	21.0	44.5	48.8	45.0
71	Power Gen. Machinery and Equipment	1.6	4.4	5.7	3.5
72	Machinery Specific by Industry	0.6	0.5	9.3	3.0
73	Metalworking Machinery	0.1	*	1.3	0.9
74	Industrial Machinery and Equip., NES	0.6	2.7	6.8	5.1
75	Office Machines and Data Processors	0.8	2.8	2.2	2.9
76	Telecommunications	7.5	9.7	3.7	4.8
77	Electrical Machinery and Parts	7.3	15.3	6.7	14.5
78	Road Vehicles	2.1	8.8	9.6	8.7
79	Other Transportation Equipment	0.5	0.2	3.5	1.7
8	Misc. Manufactured Articles	7.9	10.1	6.6	10.3
81	Plumbing, Heating, Lighting Fixtures	0.2	0.4	0.1	0.2
82	Furniture and Parts Thereof	0.4	1.9	0.2	1.0
83	Travel Goods, Handbags	0.3	0.2	*	0.1
84	Articles of Apparel, Clothing Accessories	2.5	2.2	1.4	1.6
85	Footwear	0.5	0.6	*	0.3
87	Scientific, Controlling Instruments	0.6	1.7	2.1	2.7
88	Photographic Equip., Watches, Clocks	0.2	0.3	0.8	0.6
89	Misc. Manufactured Articles, NES	3.1	2.7	2.0	3.9
9	Commodities and Transactions, NES	3.2	4.5	2.3	5.1
	Total in Millions of U.S. Dollars	$8,994.0	$27,442.1	$9,444.8	$24,018.9

* = less than 0.05 percent.

Source: OECD, *Foreign Trade by Commodities: Series C.*

to Canada in exchange for various manufactured goods, especially machinery and transportation equipment. Now the reverse is true.

By the late 1980s, Mexican exports were increasingly dominated by electrical power generating equipment, office machinery and computers, telecommunications equipment, automotive products, and other industrial machinery and transportation equipment. Meanwhile, Canadian sales were increasingly dominated by food and raw materials (see Table 4).

CONCLUDING REMARKS

The structure of Mexico's trade with both the United States and Canada continues to be influenced by the legacy of Mexico's import-substitution policies as well as by U.S. and Canadian trade policies. Much of the recent growth in Mexican exports to the United States and Canada has been in telecommunications, electrical machinery, automotive products, and various other industrial machinery. Areas of traditional strength for economies at Mexico's stage of development—apparel, basic steel and many basic consumer goods—so far have not played a major role in the recovery of the Mexican economy.

Mexican accession to the GATT and the bilateral accords negotiated since 1985 as well as Mexican economic reforms have played some role in reducing the barriers to a structure of trade that would more accurately reflect the three countries' comparative advantages. However, many barriers remain, both real and psychological. With regard to the latter, the full effect of Mexican economic reforms will not be felt until foreign investors are confident that these reforms are permanent and access to the U.S. market is assured.

What does this tell about the likely effects of the proposed free trade agreement? First, Mexico has considerable latent competitive advantages in labor-intensive industries such as apparel—the export surge that would result from free access to the U.S. and Canadian markets would impose burdensome adjustments on many U.S. and Canadian workers and communities dependent on these industries. Second, Mexico's export drive will not be limited to these sectors. More technologically intensive industries such as automotive products have become increasingly entrenched in the Maquiladora region. Mexico's export drive will become increasingly broad-based, and free trade would exacerbate the resulting adjustments in U.S. and Canadian labor markets. These adjustments are discussed in the next chapter.

TABLE 4
DISTRIBUTION OF CANADIAN TRADE WITH MEXICO, 1979 AND 1988
(Percent)

SITC		Imports 1979	Imports 1988	Exports 1979	Exports 1988
0	Food and Live Animals	43.5	8.7	15.1	20.7
1	Beverages and Tobacco	2.1	1.0	*	0.1
2	Crude Materials, Inedible, except Minerals	11.7	5.6	19.5	30.8
3	Mineral Fuels, Lubricants and Related Products	*	4.7	2.0	0.6
32	Coal, Coke and Briquettes	*	*	2.0	0.6
33	Petroleum and Related Products	*	4.7	*	*
34	Gas, Natural and Manufactured	*	*	*	*
4	Animal and Vegetable Oils, Fats, Waxes	*	*	0.5	0.4
5	Chemicals and Related Products, NES	3.6	1.2	5.0	4.3
51	Organic Chemicals	1.1	0.4	0.2	*
52	Inorganic Chemicals	1.3	*	1.3	0.1
53	Dyeing, Tanning, Coloring Materials	*	*	*	*
54	Medicinal, Pharmaceutical Products	0.9	0.4	0.4	0.3
55	Essential Oils, Perfumes, Soaps, Cleansers	*	0.1	0.1	*
56	Fertilizers, Manufactured	*	*	0.6	3.0
57	Explosives, Pyrotechnic Products	*	0.2	*	0.3
58	Artificial Resins and Plastics, Ethers	0.2	*	2.2	0.2
59	Chemical Materials and Products	*	0.1	0.2	0.3
6	Manufactured Goods Classified by Mat.	8.6	8.2	19.6	13.8
61	Leather and Furskins	0.4	*	*	*
62	Rubber Manufactures	*	*	0.3	0.6
63	Cord and Wood Manufactures	0.2	*	*	*
64	Paper, Paperboard, Articles of Pulp	*	0.3	4.2	1.9
65	Textile Yarns, Fabrics, NES	5.0	2.6	0.3	0.7
66	Nonmetallic Mineral Manufactures, NES	0.7	1.3	1.3	0.2
67	Iron and Steel	0.5	2.2	12.0	8.9
68	Nonferrous Metals	0.1	0.5	0.5	0.4
69	Manufactures of Metals	1.5	1.2	1.1	1.2
7	Machinery and Transport Equipment	21.2	66.4	33.8	26.5
71	Power Gen. Machinery and Equipment	0.7	20.0	5.8	3.4
72	Machinery Specific by Industry	0.6	0.1	7.5	1.5
73	Metalworking Machinery	0.3	*	1.5	0.0
74	Industrial Machinery and Equip., NES	0.5	4.0	3.5	2.2
75	Office Machines and Data Processors	1.9	7.7	3.4	2.6
76	Telecommunications	7.9	6.1	1.3	1.1
77	Electrical Machinery and Parts	2.7	13.3	3.2	3.4
78	Road Vehicles	6.5	15.2	6.4	10.4
79	Other Transportation Equipment	0.2	*	1.2	1.0
8	Misc. Manufactured Articles	8.4	3.4	4.5	1.2
81	Plumbing, Heating, Lighting Fixtures	1.2	0.6	*	*
82	Furniture and Parts Thereof	0.1	0.6	*	0.2
83	Travel Goods, Handbags	0.2	*	*	*
84	Articles of Apparel, Clothing Accessories	1.8	0.4	0.1	0.1
85	Footwear	0.8	0.2	*	*
87	Scientific, Controlling Instruments	0.1	0.1	2.7	0.5
88	Photographic Equip., Watches, Clocks	0.2	0.1	1.5	0.1
89	Misc. Manufactured Articles, NES	4.1	1.2	0.1	0.4
9	Commodities and Transactions, NES	1.0	0.8	*	1.5
	Total in Millions of U.S. Dollars	$177.9	$1027.5	$201.4	$398.9

* = less than 0.05 percent.

Source: OECD, *Foreign Trade by Commodities: Series C.*

NOTES

1. For example, the provisions regarding its agricultural policies and industrial policies in automobiles, pharmaceuticals and electronics.

2. As a developing country, Mexico enjoys special and more favorable treatment as provided by Part IV of the GATT.

3. As required by the GATT, U.S. and Canadian laws require that subsidized imports impose or threaten *material* injury on an established industry or *materially* retard the establishment of a domestic industry. Mexican law requires only that the practice in question injure domestic production or hinder the establishment of an industrial activity. For a complete review of Mexican subsidy/countervailing and antidumping duty laws, see USITC, *Review of Trade and Investment Measures by Mexico*, USITC Report No. 2275 (April 1990), pp. 4–12 – 4–17.

4. Ibid.

5. Ibid., pp. 4–17 – 4–18.

6. Although it should be noted that the spread between Mexican and U.S. prices has narrowed in recent years.

7. USITC Report No. 2275, p. 4–21.

8. These included textiles, agriculture, steel, electronic products, investment, intellectual property, services, and the application of U.S. trade laws.

9. Government of Mexico, Office of the President, *Toward a Mexico-U.S. Free Trade Agreement* (1990), p. 28; and Government of Mexico, *The Mexican Agenda* (October 1990), p. 40.

10. If imports that enter under the Maquiladora program and Generalized System of Preferences are removed from the computations, U.S. and Canadian average tariffs rise to about 6 and 11 percent, respectively. See Peat Marwick Policy Economics Group, *The Effects of a Free Trade Agreement Between the U.S. and Mexico* (New York, 1991), p. 6, and Department of Finance, "Canada and a Mexico-United States Trade Agreement," Working Paper (Ottawa, July 1990), p. 7.

11. USITC, *Review of Trade and Investment Measures by Mexico*, USITC Report No. 2326 (October 1990), pp. 2–3 – 2–5.

12. The application of Canada's trade remedy laws poses similar hazards to Mexico's exports; however, owing to the small volume of bilateral trade, these laws have not attracted the same attention in Mexico.

13. USITC Report No. 2326, p. 1–3.

14. Peter Morici, "U.S.-Canada Free Trade Discussions: What Are the Issues?" *The American Review of Canadian Studies*, p. 312.

15. USITC Report No. 2275, pp. 4–3 – 4–4.

16. USITC Report No. 2275, p. 4–3, and No. 2326, pp. 2–8 and 2–16; and USITC, *The Likely Impact on the United States of a Free Trade Agreement with Mexico*, Report No. 2352 (February 1991), pp. 1–2 – 1–3.

17. *Report on Free Trade* (March 11, 1991), p. 2.

18. USITC Report No. 2326, pp. 2–8 and 1–2.

19. USTIC Report No. 2352, p. 4–43.

20. USITC Report No. 2326, pp. 2–8 and 2–23.

21. USITC Report No. 2326, p. 1–2.

22. USITC, *The Effects of Greater Economic Integration Within the European Community on the United States: Second Followup Report,* USITC Report No. 2318 (September 1990), p. 15–3—emphasis added.

23. For example, the 1991 agreement to control acid rain.

24. Ibid.

25. For example, see Leslie Kochan, *The Maquiladoras and Toxics: The Hidden Costs of Production South of the Border* (Washington, AFL-CIO, 1990); and *USITC Report No. 2326,* pp. 1–11 – 1–12.

26. Bruce Tomaso and Richard Aim, "Economy vs. Ecology, Mexico's Drive for Growth Eclipses Concerns About Toxic Waste from the Border" (Transboundary Resource Report, Spring 1990), p. 2.

27. Chris Kraul, "A Warmer Climate for Furniture Makers," *Los Angeles Times* (May 14, 1990), p. D4.

28. See Peter Morici, "The Environment for Free Trade," "The Implications for U.S. Policy" and "Living with Free Trade" in *Making Free Trade Work: The Canada-U.S. Agreement* (New York: Council on Foreign Relations), pp. 10–12, 129–131 and 166–167.

Adjusting to Free Trade

4

According to economic theory, the benefits and adjustment costs created by a free trade agreement, if achieved, would emanate from two sources.

First, free trade would permit greater specialization and a more efficient allocation of continental physical and human resources—the United States and Canada would exchange low-technology/skilled goods and jobs for high-technology/skilled goods and jobs. In addition, climatic and resource advantages in agriculture and extractive industries should permit additional specialization.

In the United States, this would lower the costs of many items to consumers and raise the incomes of firms and workers in advanced telecommunications equipment, industrial machinery, and pharmaceuticals and their intermediate chemical inputs, as well as growers of grains and oilseeds. These gains would come at the expense of firms and workers, for example, in apparel, consumer electronics and automotive products, and winter vegetables and citrus fruits (more on this below). Although most empirical studies of trade liberalization, such as studies of the EC experience, indicate that the sum of the income gains to the "winners" are greater than the sum of the costs to the "losers," free trade would clearly redistribute income among classes of workers.

Second, free trade could be expected to accelerate Mexican economic growth, creating a larger market for U.S. goods and services and thereby increasing the benefits of the "winners" and decreasing the adjustments imposed on the "losers."

A real problem for policymakers is that many of the benefits of free trade in a continental economy are broadly spread—lower costs for consumers and producers in many sectors—while adjustment costs tend to be highly focused within subsectors of the economy. Moreover, economists generally view adjustment costs as transitory and declining with time and benefits as enduring and increasing over time. How policymakers evaluate free trade really depends on how they choose to balance thin but broadly based benefits to consumers and many firms and workers, on the one hand, against painful adjustments for a concentrated group of firms and workers, on the other hand.

ASSESSING THE SIZE OF BENEFITS AND ADJUSTMENT COSTS

Most empirical studies project that the benefits and adjustment costs created for the entire United States would be small because the Mexican economy is quite small compared to the U.S. economy and because both countries have already substantially reduced trade barriers. For example, in the case of the United States, consider the benefits afforded Mexico through the Maquiladora program and the Generalized System of Preferences, as well as low U.S. tariffs in many sectors. In the case of Mexico, consider the substantial economic reforms described in Chapter 2.

The INFORUM modeling group estimates that free trade would increase U.S. GNP two-tenths of 1 percent and lower Mexican GNP three-tenths of 1 percent. It would increase U.S. imports and exports by 0.4 and 1.6 percent and increase Mexican imports and exports by 4.1 percent and 20 percent. The United States loses the most jobs to Mexico in apparel—about 7,200 or less than 1 percent of 1989 employment.[1] Similarly, the International Trade Commission concluded that the likely benefits to the U.S. economy and the net effects on individual sectors of the economy would be modest.[2]

If these estimates are in the same time zone as the likely outcomes of free trade, why is President Salinas willing to go to

TABLE 5
COMPOSITION OF FOREIGN DIRECT
INVESTMENT IN MEXICO, 1983–89
(Percent)

a. Country of Origin	
United States	62.1
Great Britain	7.3
Germany*	6.6
Japan	5.5
Switzerland	4.2
France	3.1
Others	12.2
b. Major Sector	
Agriculture	0.1
Mining	1.5
Manufacturing	66.8
Services	31.6

*Federal Republic of Germany.

Source: U.S. Embassy, *Foreign Investment Climate Report* (June 1990).

such great lengths to achieve free trade in the first place? The answer is that the benefits and adjustment costs for the Mexican and U.S. economies should be much larger than empirical studies indicate for several reasons.

First, the full impact of Mexico's economic reform program has not yet been felt by its industrial structure and the export competitiveness of its industries. For one thing, indigenous Mexican investors have wisely been cautious about making long-term commitments without seeing what will be the final terms of access to the U.S. market and scope of competition from U.S. products in the Mexican market. For another, foreign investors have also been wise to be cautious about entering Mexico, owing to concerns about the permanence of economic reforms. The "announcement" effect of free trade would likely create a rush of U.S., Japanese and European investment, with significant consequences to U.S. firms and workers in industries vulnerable to inexpensive Mexican labor

Assessments of the likely effects of free trade that seek only to quantify the effects of the trade barriers remaining on paper miss much of the dynamic adjustment that would occur in Mexico. Free trade would codify and memorialize the economic reforms put in place since 1985, and it would actualize their consequences for the expectations and actions of foreign investors.

TABLE 6
DISTRIBUTION OF U.S. DIRECT INVESTMENT
IN MEXICO, 1989
(Percent)

Manufacturing	82.5
Food Processing	6.6
Chemicals	21.3
Metals	3.8
Machinery	4.5
Electrical Equipment	6.4
Transportation Equipment	21.4
Other	18.5
Petroleum	0.1
Banking	5.6
Wholesale Trade	n.a.
Other Financial	1.8
Services	2.0
All Other	n.a.

Source: *Survey of Current Business* (August 1990), p. 64.

Second, although the United States admits about 45 percent of its imports from Mexico at reduced duty rates through the Maquiladora program, it is important to recognize that the Maquiladoras did not become so important in the Mexican export equation because U.S. barriers to most other Mexican exports were so high. Rather, they became important because the development of export-oriented production in the traditional Mexican economy was blocked by aggressive trade and industrial policies emphasizing import substitution. Historically, the greatest impediments to Mexican exports have not been U.S. tariffs and nontariff barriers but the constraints, inefficiencies and capital flight caused by Mexico's import barriers, excessive regulation of private transactions and nationalist industrial policies, as well as by foreign perceptions of the insecurity of property rights.[3]

Consider, for example, the consequences for the automotive, electronics and pharmaceutical sectors. In these and other industries, the effect of free trade would not be to eliminate substantial U.S. barriers to Mexican exports but to create an environment in which the dismantling of Mexican obstacles to export-oriented production may continue.

Third, focusing on the Maquiladoras, the managers of these mostly U.S. plants currently have strong incentives to import parts from the United States. These incentives would disappear with free trade, and managers would be freer to source lower-cost parts in Asia and Europe when they are available.

Moreover, as discussed in Chapter 2, many Japanese and European firms, for example in the automotive and electronics sectors, would be in a much better position than their U.S. counterparts to take advantage of the production opportunities in Mexico created by free trade. These firms might be more inclined to purchase producer durables and components from traditional suppliers in their home market. To the extent that they did so, the resulting bilateral exchange of low-technology/skilled goods and jobs for high-technology/skilled goods would not materialize. For example, Mexico could end up purchasing technology-intensive, high-skilled products, such as machine tools and engine parts, from Japan to make trucks and then export these vehicles to the United States.

Many analysts argue that rules of origin, such as those embodied in the Canada-U.S. FTA, would be adequate to minimize such problems.[4] However, rules of origin have no effect on purchases of capital equipment.[5] With regard to components, FTA rules of origin are not that strict. In most areas, all that is required is that materials be transformed in a physically or commercially significant way, which generally is defined to be enough value added to warrant a change in tariff classification.[6]

A trade agreement with Mexico could embody much stricter rules of origin—for example, a 50 percent North American content requirement. However, it is important to recognize that U.S. MFN tariffs average only about 6 percent and would likely be cut to about 4 percent if the Uruguay Round is successfully completed. Except in a few selected products, these tariffs are not now a principal barrier to Mexican exports.

Mexico continues to impose performance requirements on foreign investors, and Mexican officials have stated that they are interested in investment, be it from Japan or the United States, that creates employment. Although it may serve Mexican interests to look more favorably on foreign investment projects that source parts and maximize employment in Mexico, it does not serve Mexican interests to insist that parts not sourced in Mexico be sourced in the United States, as opposed to Japan, Europe or elsewhere.

Certainly, U.S. firms would have an advantage in the Mexican market as a result of tariff-free access, but Mexican tariffs are no longer high enough to make a profound difference, especially in areas where Mexican manufacturers cannot meet domestic needs. If Japanese MNCs—who demonstrated their deep pockets for new plants and R&D during the 1991 recession—were to rush into Mexico, a new triangular trade could emerge. Japan would supply Mexico with capital goods and sophisticated parts, Mexico would ship consumer goods to the United States, and the United States would send more claims on U.S. assets to Japan.

Economists are accurate to argue that should such a pattern of trade emerge, the increase in the U.S. trade deficit would be corrected by other market adjustments—especially through exchange rate depreciation and changes in domestic relative prices and wages.[7] But if these adjustments are necessary because of shortages of skilled workers, capital and technology in the United States, it is necessary to ask what the adjustments would be. The answer lies in asking American workers to make less technology- and skill-intensive products, and this would greatly exacerbate the adjustments imposed on many industrial workers.

The long-term consequences of this phenomenon would heavily depend on where young U.S. industrial workers' skills stand on the spectrum between Japanese and Western European workers, on the one hand, and Mexican industrial workers, on the other hand. The closer that young American industrial workers are to Mexicans, the more that free trade would push them into competing, through lower wages, for low-skilled jobs with Mexican workers and the less that free trade would cause them to specialize and compete with Japanese and European workers for high-skilled, high-wage jobs. In this context, consider the following.

- The National Assessment of Educational Progress found that only 5 to 8 percent of all 17 year-old American high school students demonstrate the skills needed to function in demanding jobs or to do college work.[8]

- A large and growing body of evidence indicates that U.S. high school students are receiving educations that are inferior to those of their peers in Japan and Western Europe. For example, in math and science, U.S. high school students lag Japanese students by more than four grade levels.[9]

- By some estimates, about one in five Americans now hired is functionally illiterate (and innumerate), implying a U.S. literacy rate of 80 percent.[10]

- Mexico claims a literacy rate greater than 80 percent.[11]

All of these facts indicate that the combination of free trade and skill shortages among young American workers would exacerbate pressures on employers to deskill jobs and rely on low-wage labor. The labor force adjustments created by free trade with Mexico may be much greater than anticipated by econometric studies.

The dilemma for the United States is that Mexico has undertaken a number of reforms that open its market to all comers, and it is now seeking preferential access to the U.S. market to sustain domestic momentum and foreign economic support for these policy changes. It is seeking a free trade agreement with the United States to convince domestic actors, flight capital and U.S. and other foreign investors that its economic reforms are permanent and that its access to the U.S. market is secure. In the process, Mexico is seeking to exchange multilateral liberalization for bilateral concessions. If the United States were to accede to such a deal, it would create a back door to unrestrained competition from the combined forces of Japanese and European skilled labor, technology and capital and inexpensive Mexican labor at a time when the U.S. economy may be least able to respond.

Many members of Congress have been wise to question how effectively the U.S. economy could adjust to free trade with Mexico. However, the large U.S.-Mexican wage disparity, though important, is not the only difficulty. The central problem is that multilateral liberalization in Mexico combined with preferential access to the U.S. market would lay bare the competitive weaknesses of the U.S. economy—specifically, the consequences of the decline of American public education for the competitiveness of young U.S. workers and the effects of a decade of deficit spending on the availability of internally generated funding for new plants, equipment, basic research, and product development. Until the United States corrects both of these domestic weaknesses, the only way it may be able to avoid large labor force adjustments and substantial downward pressures on real wages may be to seek preferential access in Mexico for U.S. goods and investment.

SECTORAL ADJUSTMENTS IN THE UNITED STATES

As noted, free trade with Mexico would create new market opportunities and impose new competition on many industries.[12] In many sectors, such as textiles and apparel, electronics and automotive products, trade would increase in both directions. However, within these industries, the workers, and sometimes the firms, that benefit from new export opportunities would not be the same as those displaced by new imports. The burdens visited on particular workers and communities would be much larger than overall net changes in industry trade balances and employment would indicate.

By sustaining and accelerating the process of modernization now under way in Mexico and eliminating most remaining U.S. barriers to Mexican imports, the U.S. industries that would be most affected include those segments of the apparel, electronics, automotive products, and other consumer goods industries in which Mexico's inexpensive and adequately educated industrial labor force can undercut American workers in low- and medium-technology activities. The U.S. industries that potentially may profit the most are those offering more technologically intensive consumer and producer durable goods and services, such as electronics, industrial machinery, pharmaceutical, scientific and precision instruments, and related industrial design and support services, as well as other financial and business services. In addition, segments of the agriculture and food products sectors would be affected.

As a legacy of Mexico's import-substitution strategy, Mexico's *textile and apparel industries* have been domestically oriented. Therefore, at the time the Multifiber Agreement was established, Mexico's share of the U.S. market was negligible and was locked in as U.S. import quotas were initially allocated, more or less, on the basis of then existing supplier relationships.

Although U.S. imports of Mexican sewn garments from the Maquiladoras have increased significantly, U.S. imports and exports with Mexico were still only about $750 million and $700 million in 1989, and Mexico's share of the U.S. market was negligible.[13]

Any estimate based on historical or existing market shares of the likely impacts of eliminating tariffs and other obstacles to bilateral trade will conclude that overall consequences for the U.S. industry would be small.[14] Such appraisals are misleading— trade has been so severely managed, by both countries, that historical data provide little guide to the future. Instead, the fundamentals of cost competitiveness must be examined.

By the standards of most other manufacturing activities, the start up costs in the *apparel industry* are not large, and factories are easily moved—especially in lines such as children's clothes and jeans, less expensive shirts, blouses, pants, and skirts for adults. With free trade, Mexico's wage advantage would compel U.S. producers to move south of the Rio Grande or face tough competition from third country investors who would seize the Mexican advantage. Potentially, this could disrupt labor markets and communities in the apparel industry in much the same way as did the migration of the northern textile industry to the American South some two generations ago.

Should the proposed free trade agreement with Mexico contain rules of origin similar to the FTA,[15] U.S. *textile mills* would remain cost competitive in Mexico in the short- and medium-run—many branches of textile production are not as mobile as most branches of apparel. However, in the long run, the viability of this industry would be challenged as well.

In the *steel industry*, U.S. imports and exports with Mexico were about $250 million and $425 million in 1989. With the expiration of voluntary restraint agreements in March 1992 and the elimination of tariffs and other nontariff barriers, U.S producers would likely face increased competition in some price-sensitive primary products, such as sheet, plate, bar, rod, wire, tubular products, and specialty steels (i.e., stainless and tool steel.)

In Mexico, U.S. producers have faced stiff tariff and non-tariff barriers—notably, for example, in the energy, construction and automotive sectors. They should see substantial new opportunities in higher value products, such as sheet products used in automobiles and appliances, tubular products for energy applications and non-flatrolled products for construction applications.

In the *automotive industry*, U.S. imports and exports with Mexico were $4.9 billion and $3.4 billion, respectively, in 1989. Should Mexican authorities permit a rationalization of its automotive sector by ending domestic content requirements, Mexico would enjoy a growing advantage in automotive parts and the assembly of cars and trucks—especially entry-level vehicles. It is important to recognize that Mexican production for export to the United States has been expanding from items requiring rather established technologies and minimal skills to increasingly include more advanced manufacturing operations, such as Ford's decision to build the Tracer in Mexico. This may reflect a shrinking skill advantage of U.S. entry-level industrial workers over their Mexican counterparts. If this trend continues, it could prove to be a precursor for other industrial sectors.

In the *electronics sector*, U.S. imports and exports with Mexico were $4.7 billion and $3.4 billion, respectively, in 1989. Free trade would help Mexico build on its growing capabilities in consumer electronics. The Maquiladora programs spurred the assembly of television receivers, components and office machines from sophisticated U.S. parts. With free trade, the Maquiladora plants should be expected to source more parts from third countries, and the Mexican electronics industry could be expected to expand into parts production and other medium-technology activities. For example, one of the more rapidly growing areas of Mexican exports has been electric power generating machinery and equipment—their share of Mexican sales to the United States grew from 1.6 to 2.6 percent from 1979 to 1989.

Turning to new U.S. opportunities, free trade and the modernization of Mexico's communications and manufacturing infrastructures offers important new opportunities in telecommunications equipment (e.g., satellite equipment, cellular systems, fiber-optics and data transmission systems, and switching systems), advanced computer equipment (e.g., sophisticated work stations, and medium-sized computers and mainframes), peripherals and software, and other sophisticated electrical machinery.

In the *industrial machinery sector*, U.S. imports and exports with Mexico were $3.8 billion and $4.8 billion, respectively, in 1989. U.S. producers in this sector would likely see the most significant new opportunities with free trade (discussed below); however, Mexico has an emerging capability in the lower end of the spectrum—industrial machinery's share of Mexican exports to the United States increased from 0.8 to 2.8 percent during the 1980s.

On the export side, U.S. producers of machinery would see substantial new opportunities as Mexico modernizes its traditional industrial sector and seeks to make up for underinvestment during the 1980s in many non-Maquiladora activities. Important opportunities should emerge for sales of machine tools and metalworking machinery, plastics making machinery (such as injection-molding, blow molding and extrusion machines), process control equipment, pollution control equipment, oil and gas exploration and development equipment—e.g., offshore equipment and state-of-the-art geological-analytical equipment[16]—and petrochemical equipment. Other areas likely to see new opportunities include food processing and hotel and restaurant equipment, construction machinery and farm implements.

In addition, opportunities for *engineering and consulting services* to build, modernize and maintain plants, as well as to establish quality control systems and employee training programs, would be strong in sectors such as metal foundries, electronics, chemicals, pharmaceuticals, metallurgy, pulp and paper, oil and gas, and petrochemicals.

In the *chemical sector*, U.S. imports and exports with Mexico are $0.6 billion and $2.2 billion, respectively. U.S. barriers to petrochemical imports are few, and free trade would likely have little impact on the import-competing components of the chemical industry. Important caveats relate to commitments obtained from Mexico to foreswear the two-tier pricing of petroleum and natural gas and the ability of Pemex to achieve satisfactory levels of efficient investment to meet domestic needs and develop export capacity.

Passage of proposed changes in Mexico's intellectual property law would encourage new American investments in *pharmaceuticals* and high-technology chemical products, as well as patent licensing in Mexico. In turn, this would lead to additional U.S. sales of intermediate products.

In *other industrial activities*, U.S. producers would likely face more intense competition from free trade in nonferrous metals, household glassware, footwear, and leather goods. Positively affected would be segments of U.S. producers of rubber and plastic products and scientific and precision instruments.

Depending on how deeply a free trade agreement cut into the many ownership limitations and other nontariff barriers that currently constrain U.S. participation in Mexican service markets, U.S. firms could be expected to be quite competitive in *commercial and investment banking, financial services and insurance, construction and engineering services,* and a variety of *transportation and communications services.* In the communica-

tions area, the privatization of Telemex with significant participation by Southwestern Bell should facilitate sales of both U.S.
equipment and services. Also in the service sector, border retail-
ing could be hurt as Maquiladoras become less central to the
Mexican economy and prices of American goods in Mexico fall.

In *agricultural and food products,* U.S. imports and exports
with Mexico were each about $2.7 billion in 1989. Elimination of
tariff and nontariff barriers would lead to significant increases in
Mexican sales of citrus fruits, winter vegetables and canned tuna
in the United States, while American growers of temperate zone
products such as corn, sorghum, soybeans, potatoes, and beans
would gain new markets.

SECTORAL ADJUSTMENTS IN CANADA

As noted, Canada's trade with Mexico is minimal. However,
a Mexico-U.S. free trade agreement would have important competitive consequences for Canada, whether or not it chooses to
participate, owing to its dependence on the U.S. market.[17]

In a trilateral arrangement, Canadian industries could expect to face new competitive pressures in Canadian and U.S.
markets for textiles and apparel, footwear and leather products,
automotive products (especially low- and medium-technology
parts and entry level vehicles), low- and medium-technology
electrical products and nonelectrical machinery, and plumbing
appliances. Canadian firms could find new opportunities in Mexico in certain wood and paper products, agricultural and mining
machinery, urban transportation equipment (subway cars and
buses), medium- and high-technology electrical equipment and
nonelectrical machinery, construction and engineering services,
and various financial and business services.

In the agriculture and food products sector, Canada would
acquire additional market opportunities in grains, oilseeds,
beans, and meat and fish products. It would import more winter
vegetables and tropical fruits from Mexico, but these would
largely displace purchases from other locations—e.g., California,
Florida and third country suppliers.

OVERALL SCOPE OF ADJUSTMENTS

Overall, the scope of adjustments to free trade with Mexico
would be quite substantial and larger than econometric models
have predicted. The most adversely affected U.S. and Canadian
industries would likely include apparel, electronics, automotive
products, and other consumer goods. Although increased im-

ports in these sectors would be accompanied by new export opportunities within these sectors and in others, such as producer durables and manufacturing and environmental, the workers that benefit from new export opportunities often would not be the same as those displaced by imports. The costs borne by particular workers and communities would be much larger than overall net changes in industry trade and employment balances would indicate.

These factors, the superior access to technology, capital and skilled labor enjoyed by Japanese and some European MNCs, and the multilateral benefits created by many Mexican reforms, combine to create the potential for considerable additional distress in some U.S. and Canadian labor markets and for additional downward pressure on the real wages of semiskilled workers in the United States and Canada.

Overall, structuring an agreement that would provide a balance of benefits for both Mexico and the United States/Canada poses difficult challenges for negotiators. The Canada-U.S. FTA provides a point of departure for structuring such a trilateral accord. However, an agreement with Mexico would have to go beyond the provisions of the FTA to protect U.S. and Canadian interests adequately. The role of the FTA and the key issues in the negotiations with Mexico are the focus of Chapters 5 and 6.

NOTES

1. INFORUM is a modeling group at the University of Maryland. The study described here brought together an INFORUM and a Mexican multisector macroeconomic model that simulates changes in output, employment, exports, and imports on the basis of the relative price changes that would be induced by the removal of tariffs and nontariff barriers. Like many studies of this kind, this one does not simulate the effects of increased investment in Mexico induced by free trade. Less formal economic studies, such as by the Economic Policy Institute in Washington, predict larger labor market disruptions from free trade. See INFORUM, *Industrial Effects of a Free Trade Agreement Between Mexico and the USA* (College Park, Md.: March 5, 1991).

2. According to the ITC study: "The results of the Commission's analysis show that an FTA with Mexico may have moderate to significant effects on U.S. trade with Mexico in many of the industries covered [in this report]. However, these trade gains or losses, though considerable, . . . would likely have a negligible impact on production levels in most of the U.S. industries, both overall and regionally. This is because the expected gains and losses in U.S. trade with Mexico would represent a very small share of these industries' domestic production." See USITC, *The Likely Impact on the United States of a Free Trade Agreement with Mexico*, Report No. 2352 (February 1991), p. xi.

3. These perceptions were propagated by actions such as the nationalization of commercial banking in 1982 and the outright revocation of patent protection for many products in 1976.

4. USITC Report No. 2352, p. 2–5.

5. The value added created by capital equipment is treated as "domestic" without regard to the origins of the equipment.

6. The notable exceptions are automotive products (50 percent North American content is required for vehicles to move duty free) and textiles (the amount of third country fabric that may be embodied in apparel moving duty-free is limited)—see Appendix A.

7. The overall size of the U.S. trade deficit is determined by savings and investment imbalances between the United States and its principal trading partners. High Japanese savings rates, low U.S. savings rates and high U.S. federal budget deficits are major variables in this equation.

8. Educational Testing Service, *America's Challenge: Accelerating Academic Achievement* (Princeton, 1990).

9. See Commission on the Skills of the American Workforce, *America's Choice: high skills or low wages!* (Rochester, New York: National Center on Education and the Economy, 1990), and John Bishop, "Incentives for Learning: Why American High School Students Compare Poorly to Their Counterparts Overseas," Center for Advance Human Resources Studies Working Paper 89-09 (Ithaca: Cornell University, 1989).

10. Up to 65 percent of the U.S. workforce is "intermediary" literate—i.e., they can read only between the fifth and ninth grade levels. See Bill Richards, "Wanting Workers: Just as jobs are demanding more, applicants are providing less," *The Wall Street Journal* (February 9, 1990), p. R10; and Marj Charlier, "Back to Basics: Businesses try to teach their workers the three R's since schools have failed to do so," *The Wall Street Journal* (February 9, 1990), p. R14.

11. Committee for the Promotion of Investment in Mexico, *Mexico: Economic and Business Overview* (Mexico City, June 1990), p. 23.

12. Principal sources for this section were USITC Report No. 2352; IN-FORUM, *Industrial Effects;* Peat Marwick Policy Economics Group, *The Effects of a Free Trade Agreement Between the U.S. and Mexico* (New York, 1991); and U.S. Embassy in Mexico City, "Best Prospects List" (September 1990).

13. Overall, imports accounted for about 20 percent of U.S. textile and apparel consumption; Mexico's share was about one-half of 1 percent.

14. USITC Report No. 2352, pp. 4–38 – 4–41.

15. The FTA places an annual quantitative limit on the amount of offshore fabric that may be used in the production of Canadian (U.S.) apparel exported to the United States (Canada) duty free.

16. Although it is unlikely that the ban on foreign ownership of oil and gas resources will be lifted, Mexican officials are quick to point out that foreign participation in equipment sales, construction projects and consulting services are welcome. Mexico already imports more than $600 billion a

year in oil and gas machinery and equipment, and these are likely to grow rapidly under free trade as Pemex makes up for underinvestment in the 1980s.

17. Principal sources for this section were Department of Finance, *Canada and a Mexico-United States Trade Agreement* (Ottawa, July 1990); Industry, Science and Technology, *North American Trade Liberalization: Sector Impact Analysis* (Ottawa, September 1990); Investment Canada, *Canada-U.S.-Mexico Free Trade Negotiations: The Rationale and the Investment Dimension* (Ottawa, August 1990); and Royal Bank of Canada, *Mexico-U.S. Free Trade Talks* (Montreal, September 1990).

The Role of the Canada-U.S. Free Trade Agreement 5

WHY THE FTA IS IMPORTANT

The Canada-U.S. FTA provides an important point of departure for negotiations with Mexico for several reasons.

First, it covers most of the issues the United States and Canada may wish to address with Mexico and vice versa. In the FTA, the United States and Canada expanded on the progress achieved on nontariff issues in the Tokyo Round—e.g., domestic subsidies, dumping, procurement, and standards. Similarly, the FTA defines bilateral obligations in areas that were new or proved difficult in the Uruguay Round—e.g., safeguards, foreign investment, services, and agriculture. The FTA addresses these issues in ways that are broadly supportive of both regional integration and future progress in the GATT.[1] However, the FTA often addresses them in greater scope and more rigor, as is useful and perhaps only possible in a regional context, and it does so by establishing market-oriented disciplines consistent with the institutional makeup of the U.S. and Canadian economies.

Second, although trilateral negotiations could result in an agreement with Mexico that addresses a range of issues similar to those in the FTA, a trade agreement with Mexico would not likely liberalize trade and investment either as much as or as quickly as the FTA, owing to differences in U.S.-Canadian and Mexican legal and economic institutions, industrial policies and levels of development. A likely agreement with Mexico would match the FTA in "breadth" but not in "depth."

Nevertheless, it would best serve U.S. and Canadian interests for an agreement with Mexico to ascend to the FTA in both breadth and depth according to modalities and timetables established before tariff cuts began. For example, Mexico remains a substantially regulated and managed economy, constitutional considerations regarding natural resources aside. Mexican performance requirements for foreign investors, even under the new investment decrees, far and away exceed in scope and rigor the kinds of performance requirements imposed by Canada at the zenith of its economic nationalism (1980–82). It may not be reasonable to ask Mexico to dismantle all elements of these practices and conform its regulations to FTA disciplines immediately. However, by establishing FTA rules as the standard to which Mexican practices must ascend over a prearranged period, the United States and Canada would receive assurances that interventionist Mexican policies were not memorialized by an agreement.

Within the context of free trade, the maintenance of aggressive Mexican policies could easily victimize U.S. and Canadian trade and investment interests if the endurance of such practices were implicitly sanctioned by vagueness in an agreement. A trade agreement must do more than lock in the reforms that Mexico has already achieved. If the United States and Canada are to expose their labor forces and businesses to the full competitive pressures of Mexican industry and labor, then an agreement must establish a framework for bringing Mexican practices, on the full range of industrial and trade policies, within the general norms of Western industrial economies and the more rigorous and specific standards established by the FTA.

Third, should an agreement be reached with Mexico, other Latin American economies will petition to be included. Establishing the FTA as the template would set the precedent that the United States will frame its agreements in a regionally standardized fashion. This would establish the basis for a wider pluralateral trading zone, as opposed to the hub-and-spoke system of bilateral accords.

It is imperative that the United States obtain a commitment from Mexico to open its market to new partners on the same basis as the United States and thereby share in the adjustment costs of creating a hemispheric free trade area. This could be achieved by including a protocol of accession for new applicants, which should include the basis for negotiating expectations and timetables for conforming applicant practices with the disciplines of the Mexican agreement, and hence with the disciplines of the FTA. If the United States failed to persuade Mexico to accept such an approach, then the United States would risk bearing the brunt of the adjustment costs of creating a wider hemispheric free trade zone.[2]

The remainder of this chapter analyzes the provisions of the FTA that are most relevant to trade talks with Mexico and the problems that would be encountered in applying the FTA to Mexico. Although it would be desirable to have an agreement with Mexico ascend to the disciplines of the FTA, the FTA does not address many aspects of trade and industrial policy that are relevant in the case of Mexico.

GENERAL PROVISIONS OF THE FTA

The Canada-U.S. FTA is one of the most ambitious agreements establishing a free trade area under the GATT. It eliminates tariffs and most import and export measures. It extends GATT disciplines, establishes a standstill on new discriminatory practices and sets goals for follow-on negotiations on a broad range of trade and industrial policies. Among these are safeguards, standards and technical regulations, domestic subsidies and countervailing duties, crossborder dumping and domestic predatory pricing, investment, procurement, energy, automotive policies, and safeguards. The two countries have embarked on an agenda that is almost as ambitious as the EC 1992 program.

Indeed, in many ways, the United States and Canada are committed to creating an economic community, less a common external tariff and a central governing body.[3] In this section, some of the provisions relevant to negotiations with Mexico are discussed. Appendix A contains a more rigorous summary of the FTA.

Tariffs and Border Measures

The FTA phases out all tariffs by 1998, eliminates virtually all import quotas and prohibits export taxes, the dual pricing of exports and most export restrictions.

Rules of origin require that goods be transformed in a physically or commercially significant way to qualify for duty free treatment.

With regard to export restrictions in times of shortages or crisis, available supplies must be allocated on the basis of historic consumption patterns.

Safeguards

The FTA establishes rules for bilateral safeguard actions, taken in response to the effects of FTA tariff cuts, and for global safeguard actions as well.

Until January 1, 1998, tariffs may be restored for as long as three years should domestic producers suffer serious injury as a result of bilateral tariff reductions. In each industry, tariffs may be restored only once. The single exception is horticultural products. To ease the transition for Canadian fruit and vegetable farmers, tariffs may be briefly reinstated during periods of depressed market conditions for up to 20 years.

Focusing on global actions, each country will exempt the other from GATT Article XIX safeguard actions in situations where the other is *not* a substantial source of injury (i.e., more than 5 to 10 percent of imports). In such case, imports may not be reduced below their trend "over a reasonable base period with allowance for growth."[4]

Product Standards

Each country will continue to define its own product standards, which may be stricter in one country; however, the United States and Canada are committed to making standards more compatible and harmonizing them where appropriate, so that products do not have to be made differently to be sold in both countries. The two federal governments will recognize each other's national testing facilities and certification bodies and encourage private testing laboratories (e.g., Underwriters Laboratories) to accept one another's test data.

Subsidies and Dumping

The United States and Canada agree to develop by 1995 "more effective rules and disciplines concerning the use of government subsidies" and "unfair pricing"[5] (dumping and predatory pricing in an antitrust sense). In the interim, the two governments will continue to apply existing national laws. To assure Canada (the United States) that the U.S. International Trade Commission and the Department of Commerce (Canadian Department of National Revenue and International Trade Tribunal) are applying these laws rigorously, the agreement replaces judicial review of their findings by binding review by binational panels. These panels examine whether agency findings are "in accordance with the antidumping or countervailing duty law of the importing country."[6]

Procurement

The FTA lowers the threshold for purchases covered by the GATT procurement code from $171,000 to $25,000, a limited achievement as the code applies to federal purchases and not to procurement by the states and provinces.[7] The two governments agree to expand the FTA provisions regarding procurement within one year of the conclusion of the Uruguay Round.

Notably for talks with Mexico, the GATT code does not apply to the purchases of state-owned enterprises.

Energy

Due to Mexico's constitutional limitations on foreign participation in the energy sector, it is important to be clear about what the FTA does and does not do. Canada brings to the negotiating table many of the same concerns as Mexico regarding energy, although these are not constitutional matters in Canada. With the exception of the FTA's pricing provisions, Mexico could probably accede to its provisions with only technical adjustments.

Under the FTA, Canada reserves the right to screen and exclude new U.S. ownership in oil and gas exploration and development. It is not required to contract to sell oil and gas to the United States; it is only required to honor those contracts once signed and to share available supplies on the basis of recent consumption patterns in the event of shortages and emergencies (see Appendix A).

Regarding pricing, FTA prohibitions on export taxes and the dual pricing of exports require that Canadians sell Americans petroleum and natural gas at the same prices paid by Canadians under comparable commercial circumstances.

Mexican officials have indicated that they wish to phase out the dual pricing of energy products—i.e., lower prices for petrochemical feedstocks. Moreover, Mexico has negotiated with the United States on energy prices in the past—it did so in the 1985 Understanding on Subsidies and Countervailing Duties (see Chapter 3).

Automobiles

All duties on automobiles and parts are being phased out for producers that meet a strict 50 percent U.S.-Canadian content rule. In addition, Canada, under grandfathered provisions of the Automotive Agreement of 1965, continues to admit duty free the captive (third country) imports of General Motors, Ford, Chrysler, and Volvo (see Appendix A).

As a result of these provisions, the structure of Mexican tariffs, the Maquiladora program, and the structure of foreign investments in Mexico, most automotive products pass between the United States/Canada and Mexico duty free.[8]

Agriculture

In agriculture, the trade problems created by farm support programs require multilateral solutions; however, the FTA takes some positive steps. Export subsidies in bilateral trade are prohibited, and Canada agreed to remove import restrictions on U.S. wheat, oats and barley when U.S. support levels were lowered to Canadian levels. Both countries are now exempt from each other's red meat import laws. However, U.S. import restrictions on sugar-containing products and Canadian quotas on poultry and eggs are moderated only slightly, and both countries' dairy programs are largely unaffected.

Of significance to the talks with Mexico, Canada agreed to limit seasonal tariffs that essentially disadvantaged U.S. growers when Canadian horticultural products were in season. However, to ease the transitions for Canadian growers, the 20-year snapback provisions for tariffs were included in the agreement.

In agriculture, food and related products (e.g., seeds, pesticides and veterinary drugs), the United States and Canada are seeking to create an "open border" by completely harmonizing technical regulations and inspection procedures.

Investment

Chapter 16 of the FTA is a comprehensive agreement governing the treatment of foreign investment outside the financial sector. Financial services are addressed less formally elsewhere in the agreement. Exempt from the provisions of Chapter 16 are U.S. ownership restrictions in the communications and atomic energy sectors and Canadian restrictions in the communications, oil and gas, uranium, and cultural industries.

Once established, the United States and Canada will afford each other's businesses national treatment. Canada reserves the right to screen *direct* acquisitions of only its 100 largest nonfinancial corporations. Should the United States establish general screening of foreign investment, Canada would be exempt.

The FTA prohibits minimum national equity requirements, except in financial services and the excluded sectors noted above.

Performance requirements directly affecting bilateral trade are clearly prohibited—namely, goals for local content, import substitution, domestic sourcing, or exports. Such requirements for third country investors are also prohibited if they could have a significant impact on bilateral trade.[9]

Importantly in the context of negotiations with Mexico, the issues of performance requirements relating to R&D, technology transfers and world product mandates are left unresolved. Canadian officials maintain that such performance requirements are now accepted and legitimized because they are not prohibited by the FTA. U.S. officials do not share this view.

Business Services

With regard to *new* practices and regulations affecting business services, the United States and Canada will afford each other's firms national treatment and right of establishment, and they will recognize the need for compatible licensing and certification requirements. In services, barriers to U.S.-Canadian trade are minimal; however, the two governments have agreed to eliminate existing impediments through sector-by-sector negotiations.

The services chapter is supplemented by a chapter providing for the expedited movement of professional and technical workers for temporary employment for periods up to two years. The employees eligible for such passage are defined by a long and precise list, which the two parties occasionally amend at the request of professional groups and societies. Notably for talks with Mexico, this list does not include what are normally thought of as blue collar employees for factory, agricultural, construction, or simple manual work.

These provisions, combined with the precise rules governing foreign investment established in Chapter 11, create an overarching framework for trade in nonfinancial services.

Financial Services

FTA negotiators had to accommodate substantial differences in the regulatory structures of two federal systems—as they relate to the allocation of responsibilities between federal and state/provincial authorities; the division of activities among commercial banks, investment banks and other financial intermediaries; the cross-jurisdictional activities of commercial banks; and the treatment of foreign entities. At the time of the negotiations, Canada was taking steps that would make its system somewhat more similar and accessible to U.S. firms.

The FTA codified a number of changes in Canadian law that expanded U.S. financial institutions' access to the Canadian market, and some concessions were made by the United States to Canadian banks that did not apply to offshore banks (see Appendix A). While the FTA does not provide the kinds of broad guarantees for financial services that it does for business services, the principal remaining barriers to bilateral integration emanate more from the impact of domestic regulations on industry rationalization—e.g., U.S. constraints on interstate banking and Glass-Steagall.

As the two countries modify their regulatory environments, the Canadian Department of Finance and the U.S. Department of the Treasury will work to assure mutual benefits of access.[10]

Dispute Settlement

A Canada-United States Trade Commission, composed of the two countries' trade ministers, mediates disputes. When the Commission fails to achieve a mutually satisfactory resolution within 30 days, a panel of five experts may be established to make recommendations to the Commission, and their findings generally are published. Binding arbitration is available if both parties agree.

All disputed safeguard actions will be subject to binding arbitration. Disputes regarding the application of subsidies/countervailing and dumping duties are handled through a separate procedure, noted above, and its panel findings are generally binding. Disputes regarding financial services will be left to the Departments of the Treasury and Finance to work out.

PROBLEMS WITH APPLYING THE FTA TO MEXICO

Michael Hart, a Canadian FTA negotiator and noted trade policy analyst, has written persuasively that it should be possible to draft a protocol of accession to the FTA for Mexico.[11] There are some problems with specific issues such as procurement—what to do about the purchasing practices of the parastatal sector—and energy—defining the scope of activities covered by Mexico's constitutional restrictions. Such issues raise technical problems but are resolvable, and they would be with us regardless of whether negotiators used the FTA as a point of departure.[12]

However, there would be other, broader systemic challenges associated with creating and enforcing a Mexican protocol of accession or a trilateral agreement that envisioned the conduct of U.S./Canadian-Mexican commerce ascending to the disciplines of the FTA. There are specific and abiding obstacles to placing the conduct of commerce with Mexico in a market framework consistent with the norms of Western industrialized countries. Assessing these obstacles in the context of the FTA places in vivid relief the vexing challenges of achieving a trilateral or bilateral agreement that would truly elevate commerce with Mexico to the same plane as U.S. commerce with Canada, or even France or Italy, without regard to the role, if any, ultimately assigned to the FTA.

To make the FTA work, the United States and Canada have placed considerable trust in their shared legal traditions, economic institutions and experiences in the GATT because circumstances and common sense required them to do so.

To create a free trade area, the FTA had to reach deeply into the domestic management of both economies—e.g., establish understandings concerning product standards, certification of professionals and rules governing predatory pricing. To create a single market for goods, services and capital, it was necessary to take steps to ensure that domestic practices could not inadvertently undermine (or be used by future governments to block) the benefits of eliminating border measures. Getting all of this down on paper, correctly, in one pass of negotiations and without intruding further than would be necessary into sovereign prerogatives would have been an impossible task. Therefore, in many areas the FTA establishes general commitments and sets ambitious goals for continued liberalization and harmonization. In most areas, the time frame is not specified.[13]

What makes all of this work, however, is a common understanding among U.S. and Canadian officials and broader trade policy communities about what those commitments and goals mean and about what constitutes best efforts. These preconditions are just not present in the U.S./Canadian-Mexican context in the way they are in the U.S.-Canadian context.

For example, regarding subsidies, the United States and Canada have very similar GATT-based countervailing duty laws. Their interim agreement on subsidies, which some observers believe may become permanent, essentially uses bilateral panels to ensure that these laws are faithfully applied. This requires lawyers, retired judges and occasionally economists to certify that agency findings are in accordance with relevant statutes, legislative histories, regulations, administrative practices, and judicial precedents. Panels have essentially been examining agency findings to ensure that they are based on the faithful application of the law and sound economic analysis. The system works because the U.S. and Canadian trade law and international economic communities have a long heritage of jointly interpreting and applying these laws and transferring their experiences and concepts of correctness from one national context to other.

Mexico has established similar subsidy/countervailing duty laws, but its lawyers and economists have not yet had the opportunity to develop an adequate base of experience in applying the law in the context in which markets, not governments and monopolists (see below), are the arbiters of price. If, for example, an agreement with Mexico were to embody the FTA mechanism for evaluating subsidy/countervailing duty findings and the Department of Commerce found that some future Pemex pricing scheme affords petrochemical producers a feedstock subsidy, it would take a bold leap of faith for the U.S. industry to entrust review of that finding to a U.S./Mexican panel if the fifth panelist was a Mexican.[14] It is important to be clear on this point—Mexican integrity and earnest intentions are not the issue; perspective and experience are.

Turning to dumping, U.S. and Canadian negotiators have come to the conclusion that in a single market a common approach to predatory pricing should replace dumping laws. This is their goal for ongoing negotiations. Their antitrust laws draw somewhat different boundaries but are based on common concepts about fairness in pricing, collusion and the efficacy of markets; Canadian and U.S. antitrust lawyers think in the same terms and move with considerable agility between the two national legal contexts. Mexican monopoly law, like many aspects of the Mexican legal and economic systems, is premised on government management and regulation of the economy and on the concept of import substitution as a primary goal and much more important than market efficiency.

According to Alejandro Junco, editor of *El Norte:*

> The monopoly laws of Mexico date back to a time when the government was more interested in intervening in the economy and in controlling markets than in encouraging equal opportunity. The 1934 law currently in use encourages price fixing and government intervention and discourages imports. In fact, as a starting points, the law states as prima facie: "being as it is more evident that states should intervene in the economy . . . and that the market cannot be left to the free play of individuals and that markets must be regulated to reach adequate levels of pricing. . . ." Furthermore, Article VI exempts a company from being accused of monopoly practices if the government owns stock . . . whereas importing "disloyal" products *is* considered a monopoly practice.
>
> *In most Mexican markets competitive pricing is the result of either unilateral management policy or government controls.*[15]

According to Junco, monopolies and duopolies control the following in Mexico: petroleum, telephone and data communications, television broadcasting, bread, cement, steel, cookies, glass, railroads, beer, copper, baby food, and many other products and services.

The Salinas Administration is earnest in its desire to change the way the economy is run. However, in areas where it has moved—such as regulations and investment—it has not changed laws, but issued presidential decrees. Moreover, even if the laws could be changed overnight, what could not be changed overnight are the traditions, customs and ethos. These are important elements in the successful chemistry of the Canada-U.S. FTA.

Proponents of a free trade agreement point out that an agreement with the United States would bind the Mexican government in areas such as foreign investment where it has issued decrees. However, unless a trade agreement got down to the specific details of internal domestic policies, such as antitrust, deregulation and standards, and the purchasing practices of parastatal corporations and government-sanctioned monopolies, it might not have an adequate impact on a great body of law and ingrained customs that discriminate against foreign investors and imports.

Put differently, for a trade agreement to truly liberalize the management of Mexico's economy and its commerce with the United States and Canada, mere Mexican accession to the FTA, as ambitious as that would be, would not be enough.

NOTES

1. In particular, FTA disciplines are consistent with established GATT rules, and the agreement is designed to permit the United States and Canada to move forward on bilateral issues where the GATT cannot currently make progress without impeding U.S. and Canadian participation in future GATT negotiations.

2. The concerns described in this paragraph would apply equally to Canada if Canada were to join the United States in opening its market to a succession of Latin American countries without Mexico's direct participation.

3. The absence of a common external tariff does not have the significance it would have had when the EC was established because tariffs now play a much smaller role in trade policy. With the apparent failure of the Uruguay Round, though, the absence of a central governing body may prove more critical. With regional blocs becoming the primary focus of trade negotiations and the framework for development of trade policy, explicitly in the EC and implicitly in East and Southeast Asia, the United States and Canada may now have the means to bring down barriers to their bilateral trade, but they lack an effective framework to respond jointly to the sectoral predation that may well characterize a regionally oriented, post-Uruguay multilateral system.

4. FTA Article 1102, paragraph 4.b.

5. FTA Article 1907, paragraph 1.

6. FTA Article 1904, paragraph 2.

7. The EC has pressed very hard in the Uruguay Round to extend coverage to subnational governments.

8. See Industry, Science and Technology Canada, *North American Trade Liberalization: Sector Impact Analysis* (Ottawa, September 1990), p. 8.

9. FTA Article 1907, paragraph 2.

10. For example, should the United States repeal Glass–Steagall, Canadian financial institutions would be entitled to national treatment; the United States is not similarly bound to extend such benefits to other countries.

11. Michael Hart, *A North American Free Trade Agreement: The Strategic Implications for Canada* (Halifax: The Institute for Research on Public Policy, 1990).

12. For example, regarding procurement, the real issue is to bring U.S., Canadian and Mexican subnational governments and state–owned enterprises within the disciplines of the GATT Procurement Code for the purposes of continental trade. Given Mexico's large parastatal sector, it would not serve U.S. interests to enter into an agreement of any kind, be it a protocol of accession or a much less ambitious bilateral document, that did not include commitments for nondiscrimination and transparency in the purchasing practices of Mexico's vast, even if shrinking, parastatal sector.

   With regard to energy, although it would serve U.S. energy-security and Mexican development interests to bypass constitutional restriction regarding foreign participation, the bottom-line issue should be to circumscribe the scope of foreign ownership restrictions and limit their applicability to downstream activities—e.g., basic and secondary petrochemicals; and extract a commitment from Mexico to foreswear the dual pricing of petroleum and natural gas. As noted above, Mexico has shown flexibility on the pricing issue in the past. Again, these issues are critical without regard to whether we are talking about a protocol of accession to the FTA or a limited bilateral agreement.

13. Subsidies, dumping and government procurement are the notable exceptions.

14. The United States and Canada each choose two members of FTA panels. These four pick a fifth panelist. If they cannot agree, the fifth member is chosen by lot.

15. Alejandro Junco, "The Case for an Internal Mexican Free Trade Agreement," *The Wall Street Journal* (March 22, 1991), p. A9—emphasis added.

Issues in the Negotiations

6

The issues confronting the United States in negotiations with Mexico are best delineated in the context of broader U.S. goals vis-a-vis Mexico, the global competitive position of U.S. industry and labor, and the distinctive institutional frameworks that define the processes of consolidation of regional trading blocs in North America and Asia.

THE BROADER CONTEXT

In Mexico, the United States seeks to contribute to an environment that will help to reverse the erosion of living standards that occured after the debt crisis. Higher living standards and social justice in Mexico would translate into political stability and broader markets for U.S. and Canadian goods and services.

The United States and Canada can most effectively facilitate sustained economic progress in Mexico by encouraging Mexico to continue liberalizing its economic institutions. In this regard, U.S. and Canadian negotiators must resist a quick, limited deal—one that offers Mexico additional market access, without fully bringing the management of its economy into conformity with the norms of Western industrial nations.

A limited pact would offer Mexico only temporary economic and political benefits, the United States fleeting security benefits and Canada none of these. It would impose on the U.S. and Canadian labor forces adjustment costs without ensuring the full market access benefits to be obtained from a transformed Mexican economy. An agreement hastily conceived—to shore-up support for President Salinas—would be a risky venture.

In establishing a long-term process with Mexico, it seems imperative to remain focused on three realities.

First, a long-term process requires sustaining political support in the United States and Canada. To this end, labor market adjustments must be managed, and the competition among U.S., Canadian and Mexican communities and workers for plants and jobs must be fair.

The former requires careful phasing in of increased Mexican access to the U.S. market in import-sensitive sectors. In turn, this requires recognition that in some activities the most significant U.S. and Canadian barriers to Mexican imports are not tariffs but quantitative restrictions. In industries such as apparel, the phasing in of increased market access requires gradual relaxation of these restrictions, as opposed to eliminating them quickly and relying on the staged tariff reductions to cushion adjustments.

Establishing fair competition for investment and jobs requires dismantling Mexican industrial policies such as development programs in priority sectors and foreign investment screening and performance requirements. Equally important, it requires prompt and effective enforcement of environmental and workplace health and safety standards. American political support for free trade with Mexico will remain vulnerable as long as sweat shop conditions and lax environmental enforcement prevail in Mexico.

Second, as noted in Chaper 5, should negotiations achieve a free trade agreement with Mexico, it would likely be as broad but not as deeply cut as the Canada-U.S. FTA, at least in the short run. However, given the legacy of statist policies in Mexico, an agreement with Mexico should extend to issues that were not covered by the FTA, and the disciplines must be spelled out in greater detail than was necessary in the FTA. Only through such a process can the United States and Canada ensure that their businesses do not fall prey to predatory industrial policies that could be put in place by some future, less market-oriented Mexican government. Hence, in the long run, to fully integrate the U.S., Canadian and Mexican economies, an agreement must be broader and cut even more deeply than the FTA.

Third, although the world is moving toward three regional trading blocs, it is important to recognize that these blocs are developing in quite different competitive and institutional contexts.[1] North American economic integration is accelerating at a time when Japanese MNCs—having better educated workers, deeper pockets and superior manufacturing technologies—are better positioned to exploit some of the opportunities offered by investing in Mexico.

Moreover, in a straightforward free trade agreement, the United States and Canada would lack the leverage in Mexico of the kind Japan enjoys in East and Southeast Asia to ensure that U.S. and Canadian sales of high-technology goods in Mexico and Asia match U.S. and Canadian purchases of low-technology goods from Mexico and Asia. Specifically, Japanese MNCs would be better able to penetrate the U.S. and Canadian markets by investing in Mexico than U.S. and Canadian investors would be able to penetrate the Japanese market by investing in East and Southeast Asia. This would result in an overall imbalance of opportunities between the United States/Canada and Japan in the combined North American-East/Southeast Asian market (discussed in Chapter 7). Thus, the United States and Canada should seek preferential concessions from Mexico to ensure that the benefits of free trade are balanced.

SPECIFIC NEGOTIATING ISSUES

The challenges of phasing in adjustments, encouraging the transformation of Mexican economic institutions and policies and obtaining preferential access to the Mexican market may be illuminated by considering some negotiating issues: tariffs, quantitative restrictions and safeguards; procurement; subsidies; dumping; foreign investment; and environment and workplace regulations standards.

Tariffs, Quantitative Restrictions and Safeguards

The phased elimination of tariffs, import licenses and other quantitative restrictions, coupled with appropriate transition mechanisms (e.g., bilateral/trilateral safeguards), would be the cornerstone of any agreement. Regarding quantitative restrictions, the United States and Canada should expect Mexico to phase out completely import licenses on nonagricultural commodities. Mexico will be looking for elimination of U.S. import restraints on apparel and steel.[2]

If the FTA experience is any guide, Mexico will be asked to continue to participate in the steel program until it is terminated, and complete liberalization in agriculture will pose daunting challenges.[3]

Turning to safeguards, the problem of cushioning adjustment in the Canada-U.S. FTA was handled largely by reducing tariffs in increments over 10 years.[4] The bilateral safeguard mechanism was not expected to be invoked frequently or play a major role.

In areas other than textiles, apparel, steel, and selected agricultural commodities subject to U.S. quantitative restrictions, the primary barriers to Mexico's exports have not been U.S. tariffs; rather, they have been the legacy of Mexico's industrial policies and an absence of investor confidence regarding the permanence of recent reforms and security of access to the U.S. market. A free trade agreement would eliminate these impediments, and phased tariff reductions would provide U.S. producers with little cushion against the adjustments imposed by Mexican competition.

The problem is how to deal with the adjustments imposed on workers in industries particularly vulnerable to competition from low-wage Mexican labor. The answer could lie in phasing in the growth of Mexican market shares and in recognizing the impact of low Mexican wages in this process.

For example, the United States and Canada could seek to have enumerated in the text of an agreement a *controlled list* of industries. In these industries, the U.S. and Canadian market shares captured by Mexican products and entering duty free would be permitted to grow no more than "G" percentage points a year—imports above this amount would be subject to preagreement (GATT-bound) tariffs. In computing permitted Mexican duty free market penetration, credit could be given for increased U.S. and Canadian sales in Mexico so that intra-industry specialization would partially compensate for the growth of Mexican sales in Canada and the United States.

U.S. and Canadian industries currently protected by quantitative restrictions (e.g., apparel and steel) or designated as particularly vulnerable to low-wage competition, could be placed on a *priority controlled list.* In these industries, imports above Mexico's duty free share would be subject to a tariff equal to "R" times the percentage difference between U.S. and Mexican wages. R could be set equal to the combined *ad valorem* protection afforded by tariffs, quotas and nontariff barriers at the time the trade agreement went into force.*

The industries placed on each list and the values of G and R would be determined in negotiations and specified in the text of the free trade agreement.

In return for accepting such a mechanism, Mexico would expect concessions on other issues—perhaps, it would seek its

---

* For example, suppose in the shirt industry, U.S. (Canadian) imports and exports with Mexico were M(b) and X(b) percent of U.S. (Canadian) apparent consumption (shipments plus imports less exports) in the base year prior to the agreement; M(b–1) and X(b–1) are similarly defined for the year prior to the base year. In year one of the agreement, duty free U.S. (Canadian) imports from Mexico as a share of U.S. (Canadian) consumption would be limited to:

$$M(1) = M(b) + G + [X(b) - X(b-1)]$$

In year n, the Mexican share would be limited to:

$$M(n) = M(b) + nG + [X(n-1) - X(b-1)]$$

In "controlled" industries, imports above M(n) would pay the GATT-bound tariff.

In "priority controlled" industries, imports above M(n) would be subject to an *ad valorem* tariff:

$$T = R [W(US) - W(Mex)] / W(US)$$

Where W(US) and W(MEX) are average manufacturing wages in the United States and Mexico.

own list of controlled industries. However, this is one way of recognizing the scope of adjustments and the impact of low Mexican wages on the structure of an agreement.

With regard to global safeguard actions that the United States, Canada or Mexico might take under GATT Article XIX, it seems reasonable to trilateralize the provisions of the FTA. Under that agreement, the United States would not apply a global action to Mexico or Canada unless either was a "substantial source of injury" (i.e., supplied more than 5 or 10 percent of imports); in any case, imports would not be reduced below their trend over "a reasonable base period with allowance for growth." This language is vague, has not yet been tested and could pose problems down the road.[5] Trilateral negotiations provide a good opportunity to tighten up these provisions.

Procurement

Procurement poses at least three sets of issues for the U.S. and Canadian negotiators. First, the parastatal sector in Mexico is so large that it cannot be ignored. It would be possible to apply the FTA procurement chapter, or some iteration of it, to Mexico, adding purchases of state-owned enterprises to the entities covered by its disciplines. The real problem would be monitoring and ensuring compliance with the transparent bidding requirements of the GATT and FTA in a government purchasing system with which many American and Canadian firms have little experience. It is important to remember that governments depend on information from their private sectors to articulate problems with regard to procurement. Further, extending GATT and FTA disciplines to state-owned enterprises means applying transparent bidding requirements to entities whose purchasing procedures are not always patterned after public agencies.

Second, Canada has many more state-owned enterprises than does the United States. Adding these to FTA coverage, either directly or through a trilateral accord, could upset the balance of procurement benefits negotiated between the two countries. Although this is certainly a workable issue, it illustrates once again how negotiations with Mexico have the potential to disturb the balance of benefits achieved in the FTA.

Third, and most perplexing, Mexico has recently privatized about 75 percent of its parastatals. For many, the old habits of offering domestic preferences may prove difficult to break. The same applies to government sanctioned monopolies and duopolies. Trade agreements generally do not offer ready answers to these kinds of cultural problems. However, a modern Western-like antitrust law and policy would help bring price and cost competition to many segments of the economy and thereby foster more competitive pricing and sourcing practices.

In U.S.-Japanese relations, adequate enforcement of Japanese antitrust laws, as it effects U.S. market access, has been a contentious problem. The time to address this kind of issue with Mexico is now, when we are considering an overall framework for commercial relations.

Subsidies

Regarding subsidies, the FTA has two essential components: negotiations to establish more effective rules and disciplines regarding government aids; and, until such new rules are put in place, binational panel review of administrative agency findings under the continuing application of national laws.

Regarding negotiations to develop more effective rules and disciplines, it would serve U.S. and Canadian interests to engage Mexico because any agreement they reach bilaterally to limit the use of subsidies would benefit Mexico by default without ensuring reciprocal benefits.[6]

Further, considering Mexico's long history of aiding industries and distorting trade in the process, it is essential that we obtain certain commitments from Mexico regarding subsidies before entering into a free trade agreement.[7]

Near the top of the list should be the pricing practices of its parastatal enterprises and government-sanctioned monopolies. Constitutional requirements, for example, that oil and gas exploration and development be reserved to Mexicans, is quite a different issue from the dual pricing of petroleum and natural gas that may be used as feedstock in basic petrochemical production. Application of the FTA requirement that U.S. and Canadian users be offered these and other commodities at the same prices as Mexicans, under comparable commercial circumstances, could resolve this issue. Also, assurances are needed that other prices set by state regulations, parastatals and monopolies will not place U.S. and Canadian firms at competitive disadvantages. Further, the United States and Canada should seek permanent commitments that Mexico will not again use the federal budget to subsidize the activities of parastatals or private firms engaged in the production of tradable goods and services.[8]

It would serve Mexico's interests to seek binational or trinational review of the subsidy and dumping findings by the Commerce Department, the International Trade Commission and their Canadian counterparts. In principle, this should not entail difficulties for the United States. However, the issue of the perspective and experience of Mexican panelists, discussed in Chapter 5, remains troublesome.

It would probably best serve U.S. interests for panels to be binational as opposed to trinational. Specifically, when the Department of Commerce and the ITC find a Mexican action to be a subsidy and cause injury, the review panel should be composed of Mexicans and Americans only and should not include Canadians.

Dumping

Observers of the FTA process have been quick to point out that in a single market dumping should become irrelevant and the effective application of predatory pricing laws should replace the use of existing dumping statutes. If the United States and Canada were to abandon their existing dumping regimes, anything more than minor changes in their existing predatory pricing laws would likely take them in the direction of a joint regime. However, it is difficult to see how Mexico could be included in such a process without radical changes in its competition law and policy.

Moreover, applying the FTA-type panels to dumping findings raises even greater questions about the perspective and experience of prospective Mexican panelists, given the orientation of Mexico's economy and the legacy of its monopoly laws. Again, it would probably best serve U.S. interests for these panels to be binational, as opposed to trinational.

Foreign Investment

Even with its significant liberalization, Mexico still reserves substantial segments of its domestic economy for state ownership and Mexican majority ownership, and Mexico still has substantial screening procedures and performance expectations for foreign investors. From an American perspective, three questions are critical.

- Mexicans assert that constitutional restrictions regarding foreign ownership are not on the negotiating table—what does their Constitution actually require?

- Outside of constitutionally restricted areas, is Mexico willing to phase out minimum domestic ownership requirements?

- Is Mexico willing to accept the limitations on foreign investment performance requirements contained in the U.S.-Canada FTA?

The application of Article 27 of the 1917 Constitution, which reserves subsoil rights to Mexican nationals, has widened over the years. For example, the oil industry was not nationalized until 1938, and majority Mexican ownership was not required in fishing until 1945, in timber until 1960 and in mining until 1961. The 1973 LFI essentially codified these and other restrictions (described in Chapter 2),[9] and it appears that Mexico City has some flexibility in the interpretation of Article 27.

Although the United States should not insist on changes in Mexico's Constitution, it seems reasonable for the United States to seek:

- a precise and limited enumeration of the specific sectors to which Article 27 applies, and for each such sector, a delineation of the maximum applicable extent of restrictions on U.S. investors;

- in all other sectors, elimination of minimum domestic equity requirements and performance requirements that affect trade and specialization,[10] as they apply to U.S. and Canadian investors;[11]

- Mexican acceptance of rights normally afforded foreign investors by Western industrialized countries and articulated in the FTA—e.g., national treatment, freedom to sell assets without prejudice among offshore, U.S./ Canadian and Mexican buyers, and freedom to repatriate profits.

An agreement embodying such commitments would require changes in Mexico's LFI but not in its Constitution.

Mexico may wish to phase in some of these commitments.[12] Such phasing in could be paired with safeguard provisions for sensitive U.S. sectors noted above.

Environmental and Workplace Standards

Regarding environmental and workplace standards, there are two points of view. On the one hand, some believe that these issues, which traditionally have not been a part of trade agreements negotiated by the United States, should be addressed in contexts other than the upcoming trade negotiations. On the other hand, other observers believe that these issues should be addressed directly in the proposed agreement, and Mexican access to the U.S. market should be made contingent on compliance with reasonable environmental and workplace standards.

As discussed in the Introduction and Chapter 3, a U.S. trade agreement with Mexico would not be just like other U.S. trade agreements. Like Canada, the proximity and intensity of U.S. commercial relations with Mexico gives the United States a stake in Mexican practices that exceeds its interests with countries outside North America. Unlike Canada, Mexico's enforcement of environmental and workplace standards is very deficient. As a developing country, it lacks the resources, and perhaps the technical expertise gained through experience, to ensure effective compliance with its laws; at times, lax enforcement has functioned like a development subsidy to attract industry.

Advocates of free trade argue that it would generate the growth and hence the resources needed to address Mexico's regulatory problems, and Mexican officials have expressed the desire to improve environmental and workplace conditions. In the context of a trade agreement, the United States and Canada would be entitled to assurances that lax standards and enforcement would not function like a development subsidy. In negotiations, they should seek to ensure that Mexico has the financial and technical resources to set and enforce adequate regulations and that it has strong incentives to follow through. To these ends, the following should be considered.

- Establish a Mexican Environmental Fund and a Mexican Workplace Safety Fund to be used to finance effective enforcement of environmental and workplace safety standards and to assist small and medium-sized businesses in retrofitting existing investments. This fund would be financed by dedicating 25 percent of the tariff revenue on U.S., Canadian and Mexican imports. Based on the 1990 volume of trade, this would come to about $1 billion the first year. The fund would decline over the transition period with tariff reductions, but so should Mexico's need for special aid.

- Establish U.S./Canadian-Mexican cooperative frameworks among the ministries and departments of labor and environment to provide Mexican officials with technical assistance in writing and enforcing regulations, training inspectors and the like.

- Establish specific timetables for environmental retrofitting and workplace changes to ensure compliance with national laws.[13]

- Establish a U.S./Canadian-Mexican working group with representatives from the ministries of environment and labor, organized labor and business to oversee the use of the Mexican Environmental and Workplace Safety Funds, monitor enforcement of environmental and workplace standards in all three countries and recommend regulatory changes to ensure compliance with standards.

- Within these mechanisms, sectoral advisory committees, with representatives from business and labor, could be established to develop environmental and workplace standards and enforcement procedures most appropriate to specific industrial circumstances.

Other Negotiating Issues

The elimination of Mexican import licenses, government procurement preferences and foreign investment performance requirements would end most aspects of sectoral programs in automobiles, pharmaceuticals and computers. However, Mexico could still impose domestic content goals in other ways—for example, as a condition for concessionary financing schemes or building permits. For this and other reasons, the proposed agreement should include a strong *national treatment clause.*

With regard to the *automobile industry,* consideration has to be given to North American content requirements. Currently, the United States and Canada have a 50 percent requirement for vehicles to qualify for duty free trade. Mexico has a 36 percent requirement for vehicles and a 30 percent requirement for parts. A combined North American content requirement of 50 or 60 percent makes sense.

Passage of the *intellectual property* legislation proposed by the Mexican government in January 1991, or some appropriate iteration of it, should be required by the agreement.[14]

Removing barriers to trade in *services* is very important to the United States and somewhat less so to Canada. Effective penetration of foreign markets generally requires that service providers be afforded national treatment, right of establishment and the ability to move personnel across borders. In the FTA, the former two requirements were met in the bodies of the investment and services chapter. A supplemental chapter dealt with the temporary movement of professional and technical personnel (defined by a rather precise list). The question arises how and where to draw the line between the movement of these workers and the broader *labor mobility* issues, which Mexico has said it will not press in FTA negotiations.

Preferential Treatment

Achieving meaningful preferential market access in Mexico would prove to be a vexing challenge for U.S. and Canadian negotiators. As discussed in Chapter 4, the traditional means for assuring preferential access has been through rules of origin, and this would likely prove ineffective. As an alternative, preferential access could be approached within the context of the transition mechanisms for foreign Mexican investment regulations.

As Mexico phases out minimum domestic equity require-ments (foreign equity restrictions) for industries outside the reach of Article 27, the United States may wish to ask Mexico for two concessions:

- a more rapid phase out of foreign equity restrictions for U.S. and Canadian investors than for offshore foreign investors;

- national treatment for U.S. and Canadian goods and services in Mexican screening of offshore investors' ap-plications for domestic content and similar goals.

The FTA provides some precedent for preferential treatment, although not as strong as the treatment proposed here.[15]

However, given the nature of investment screening pro-cesses, neither of these commitments would be easy to enforce. This illuminates a basic dilemma for American negotiators. If they were to accept the notion that the United States and Canada needed preferential access to the Mexican market, how would they get it? If rules of origin are not enough, other means would require asking Mexico to take administrative steps to discrimi-nate in favor of U.S. and Canadian goods. This is precisely the sort of meddling in market processes that the United States is encouraging Mexico to foreswear. Americans would be asking Mexico to "do unto others but not unto us."

SOME IMPLICATIONS FOR U.S. MULTILATERAL GOALS

Progress in the GATT and the maintenance and expansion of a market-driven framework for trade under the GATT remain primarily dependent on American leadership, resolve and stead-fastness. The United States should give careful consideration to how an agreement with Mexico would affect its goals for the multilateral system.

First, a trade agreement with Mexico, like the FTA, the EC and the broader European Free Trade Association, could be structured to be consistent with the GATT. However, a free trade agreement with Mexico, coupled with the FTA, the Structural Impediments Initiative and other bilateral efforts with Japan, the Caribbean Basin Initiative, and the Israeli agreement, would place much more than half of U.S. trade on a bilateral or regional track. With the addition of Mexico, the maintenance of bilateral and regional arrangements could easily displace the GATT as the primary preoccupation of U.S. policymakers and negotiators.

Second, U.S. efforts to obtain preferential access to the Mexican market by means other than rules of origin would undermine U.S. adherence to the most-favored-nation principle. This fundamental element of the GATT has already been dealt blows by the implementation of the Tokyo Round codes, the EC 1992 program, certain provisions of the FTA, and the application of managed trade agreements selectively by advanced industrialized countries.

Preferential treatment for the United States and Canada under Mexico's foreign investment regime would run completely counter to long-espoused policies of the United States, sraise alarm among trade policy purists at home and generate loud protests from officials in Japan and the EC. Although it bears mentioning that such treatment is very close to what the United States and Canada negotiated in Chapters 16 (Investment), 17 (Financial Services) and 10 (Automotive Products) of their FTA, extending such an approach to Mexico, along with perhaps tightening restraint agreements on Asian imports (discussed below), would amount to U.S. acceptance of a two-tier regional/GATT application of the MFN principle.

It could well be that the integrated regional trading bloc would replace the nation as the principal negotiating unit in the GATT and that a formalized and recognized two-tier application of the MFN principle—stronger obligations to bloc members than to other GATT members—would become a standard feature of U.S., Japanese and EC-member policies. The bloc would then become the central defining feature of the post-Uruguay Round GATT system. Concerns about Japan obtaining opportunities in Mexico that the United States and Canada do not enjoy in East and Southeast Asia indicate that this might serve U.S. interests; however, U.S. policymakers should understand the ramifications of such actions.

Third, depending on the substance of whatever agreements may yet be reached in the Uruguay Round regarding tariffs, safeguards and grey-area measures, textiles and apparel, other nontariff practices, services, investment, and intellectual property, the overlay on the GATT system of three semi-autonomous sets of regional rules for international commerce could create obstacles and disincentives for future multilateral progress.

In areas such as product standards, procurement and agriculture, regional arrangements and a regional structure of benefits could emerge that would become difficult to reorder or upset in the context of broader GATT negotiations. Consider, for example, the EC Common Agriculture Policy.

As regional agreements become wider and deeper—including more and more varied nations and disciplining a broader range of international and domestic policies—the benefits to be obtained from multilateral liberalizations, relative to those from regional liberalization, decline.

Focusing on North America, a trade agreement with Mexico would implicitly, yet concretely, limit access to the U.S. and Canadian markets for other developing countries.[16] Also, to dampen opposition in the Congress and Parliament to low-wage competition from Mexico, Washington and Ottawa may be forced to tighten restrictions on imports from other Latin American and East and Southeast Asian economies. Limiting imports from other Latin American countries would run counter to President Bush's Enterprise for the Americas program, indicating that trade relations with Asia could suffer. This would almost certainly reduce prospects for progress in the GATT.

NOTES

1. See Richard S. Belous and Rebecca S. Hartley, eds., *The Growth of Regional Trading Blocs* (Washington: National Planning Association, 1990).

2. Steel voluntary restraint agreements are scheduled to end in March 1992. If they are extended, both Mexico and Canada should want their permitted shipments raised.

3. Consider, for example, FTA provisions regarding sugar-containing and dairy products—see Appendix A.

4. Prior to the FTA, quantitative restrictions played little role in U.S.-Canadian trade outside steel and agricultural products. The United States and Canada impose quantitative restrictions in agriculture essentially to defend support prices and protect their farmers from each other's subsidies.

5. See David Richardson, "Adjustments and Safeguards," in Peter Morici, ed., *Making Free Trade Work: The Canada-U.S. Agreement* (New York: Council on Foreign Relations, 1991); and Peter Morici, *A New Special Relationship: The Free Trade Agreement and U.S.-Canada Commercial Relations* (Ottawa: Institute for Research on Public Policy, in press).

6. The current thinking is that a bilateral subsidies discipline will follow the red/yellow/green format that surfaced during the Uruguay Round. In this format, the signatories each agree that certain subsidies—either through explicit lists or rules—are prohibited (red), others are permitted (green) and still others are permitted but subject to countervail (yellow). Different injury tests and minimum thresholds of subsidization for action could apply to different categories of yellow light subsidies.

7. It is important to recognize that the U.S. government has offered subsidies to various industries, for example through the activities of the Economic Development Administration and the Chrysler bailout. Since the early 1980s, the states have been quite active and have attracted considerable attention among Canadian officials preparing for negotiations with the United States under the FTA. Although the United States may have more to gain from an exchange of commitments with Mexico and Canada regarding subsidies, U.S. officials are aware that a subsidies discipline could constrain U.S. freedom of action in the future.

8. Needless to say, there would be exceptions, as in agriculture.

9. U.S. Embassy in Mexico City, *Foreign Investment Climate Statement* (August 1990), Annex M.

10. At a minimum, prohibited performance requirements should include requirements that investors meet goals for export, import substitution and domestic value added and sourcing. Like the FTA, they should apply to all U.S. and Canadian investments and to any offshore investment that would significantly affect U.S.-Canadian sales anywhere in North America.

11. Like Canada, Mexico could seek some exceptions. For example, in the FTA, Canada maintains the right to screen acquisitions of existing businesses valued at more that Cdn.$150 million and to continue ownership restrictions in communications, oil and gas, uranium, and cultural industries.

12. There is precedent in the FTA. For example, Canada was permitted to phase out screening of indirect acquisitions over a three-year period.

13. Phase-in periods may have to vary by industry; however, these timetables should be negotiated in advance of the first tariff cuts.

14. The FTA has such a provision regarding Canadian pharmaceutical patent law and other intellectual property issues.

15. In the FTA, the United States and Canada exempt each other from most foreign investment screening but reserve the right to screen third country investments. Canada continues to do so through Investment Canada.

Also, the two countries agree not to impose domestic content, import substitution and export performance requirements on each other's investors, but they reserve the right to impose performance requirements on third country investors as long as such requirements do not distort bilateral trade or prejudice each other's interests.

16. The consequences will range beyond the effects of eliminating tariffs (which will not be large) to include the benefits Mexico will gain from greater investor confidence about security of access to the U.S. market.

Mexico will become less vulnerable than other Latin American and Asian developing countries regarding the application of U.S subsidy/countervailing and dumping duties, safeguard actions and managed trade arrangements.

A Time for Realism

The debate concerning free trade with Mexico has been couched in the extremes. Protagonists argue that Mexico offers the United States the opportunity to combine advanced technology, skilled labor and capital with a large, inexpensive Mexican labor force. They say this would permit the United States to trade low-technology/skilled goods for high-technology/skilled goods and swap low-wage jobs for high-wage jobs. They assert that the adjustments would be minimal because most U.S. tariffs are already low and because Mexican exports account for a very small share of U.S. markets.

Antagonists argue that Mexico's low wages, poor working conditions and lax environmental enforcement would attract businesses and leave many American industrial workers and communities stranded. In the end, U.S. industrial wages would plummet. Also, Japan could end up the real winner because in industries such as automobiles and consumer electronics, its MNCs have better access to the capital and technology necessary to combine with inexpensive Mexican labor to service the U.S. and Canadian markets.

There is truth in both sets of arguments. The United States can strengthen its competitiveness by opening up trade with Mexico. With Japanese and EC MNCs having ready access to Eastern Europe and East and Southeast Asia, the United States needs the opportunities for expanded markets and improved cost competitiveness offered by Mexico. However, if the United States does not manage the process of integration with Mexico properly, it places at considerable risk the jobs and living standards of workers in industries such as apparel, automotive products and electronics.

Unfortunately, we are not making much headway on how to manage the process effectively because protagonists and antagonists increasingly talk past one another. This keeps us from shaping a negotiating posture that reflects a balanced appreciation of the opportunities and the risks.

To begin the process, we must recognize that the advent of free trade negotiations with Mexico reveals some fundamental issues in U.S. trade policy. These emerge from the constraints on U.S. trade policy options created by Japanese trade policies, the projection of Japanese economic power and the ideological competition between American and Japanese models for the management of market economies.

THE NEW COMPETITION OF IDEAS

With the triumph of market capitalism, a new competition of ideas has emerged. What is the best model of market capitalism?

According to the American model of *atomistic capitalism*, governments should rely on the competitive instincts of private businesses and entrepreneurs to decipher international market signals, identify product development opportunities, raise risk capital, and generally reallocate physical and human resources from declining to emerging industries. Government assistance for collaboration among enterprises is seen as potentially suppressing competition, thereby impairing the national ability to advance to higher levels of industrial competence. The appropriate role for government is to keep the competition brisk by negotiating liberal rules for international trade, discouraging concentrations of domestic market power and avoiding subsidies to industry.

In the Japanese model of *syndicate capitalism*, industry groups such as the *keiretsu* are the principal instruments for progress. The government is seen as having a positive role to play by deciphering international market signals in parallel with business; providing aid to industry groups that band together to leverage risks in R&D; leaving undisturbed discriminatory corporate practices when they support the movement of resources into priority areas; and helping to ensure adequate markets for key industries through procurement.[1]

Japan does not protect everything, but it manages quite carefully what it buys and from whom. In its expansion of trade and investment in Asia, it has undertaken a conscious policy of increasing imports of low-technology products and creating a market for its high-technology goods and services. This policy is enforced by the customs, purchasing practices and foreign aid of its industrial groups and government. In the Japanese model of syndicate capitalism, lax antitrust enforcement and discrimination that support the movement of resources into areas of perceived competitive strength are not protectionist, but promarket—they are market-consistent policy.

THE AMERICAN DILEMMA

American industry, law and economic institutions are structured for the atomistic model, and this model might work best globally if our major competitors accepted it, but they do not.

This conflict of paradigms is at the root of American frustrations, for example, in bilateral talks with Japan concerning public works procurement and antitrust enforcement, and with the EC concerning subsidies to Airbus. This is an important reason why progress in the GATT is so difficult and painfully slow.[2]

In turn, the conflict of paradigms is a principal reason why trade talks with Mexico are at once so important and so troublesome for the United States. Substantial progress on the U.S. agenda for the Uruguay Round would have made most of the issues in talks with Mexico moot. The fissures separating the U.S. and Japanese models of market capitalism and international trade policies have quite deleterious consequences for the United States as regional trading blocs emerge in North America and Asia (discussed in the next section).

When the United States was the paramount economic power and the scope of international integration was more limited, the United States was able to absorb the consequences when its major competitors cheated at the edges. Now, because the United States has less capital to invest in new plants and technology than Japan and because there are genuine deficiencies in the educational backgrounds of young U.S. workers, U.S. policymakers have one remaining advantage in negotiations with Japan— they still control access to a larger national market. At the same time, U.S. policymakers feel compelled to acknowledge Mexican reforms for both political and competitive reasons and, in doing so, they open a back door for Japan to the U.S. market and compromise their last advantage.[3]

For Mexico, the choices are limited. Mexico needs capital and lots of it. U.S., Japanese and EC MNCs will not be fully confident about the efficacy of investing heavily in Mexico's traditional (non-Maquiladora) economy until an agreement with the United States assures market access and memorializes Mexican economic reforms to date.

The United States would not have considered initiating negotiations without an aggressive reform program well under way in Mexico. Although Mexican policymakers, like other Latin American leaders, have chosen to shed the old import-substitution model of economic development in favor of a market-oriented model of capitalism, for the time being they do not have the option of choosing between the American or Japanese models. The Americans hold the keys to the market opportunities the Mexicans need and to legitimatizing their reforms. In the long run, U.S. leverage could diminish, and Mexico could turn to Japanese- or French-style models of economic management.

REGIONALISM AND AMERICAN VULNERABILITY

Japan, the EC and the United States each have the opportunity to broaden their regional trading arrangements and trade low-skilled, low-wage jobs for high-skilled, high-wage jobs. Importantly, though, Japan and the EC can, if they choose, manage the process and thereby maximize market opportunities and minimize labor market disruption. The United States could easily forsake this option in trade negotiations with Mexico and make itself very vulnerable to Japanese competition.

With regard to Japan in East and Southeast Asia, it is important to recognize that the tariffs or formal quotas do not pose much of a barrier to the Japanese market for manufactured products. The problem of access is imbedded in the procurement customs of private and government entities and distribution networks. Hence, as Japan invests heavily in East and Southeast Asia, it forges a trading bloc in which it enjoys very strong preferences.

Specifically, when Japanese MNCs access cheap labor in other Asian economies, the products created by this labor gain access to the Japanese market through the distribution networks of Japanese MNCs. The producer durables and other technology-intensive components and services required by this production are purchased from traditional sources in Japan, often from within the *keiretsu.* A regional balance of opportunities is enforced through private management.

In this context, U.S. and Canadian MNCs cannot access inexpensive labor in Asia to penetrate the Japanese market with the same ease that Japanese MNCs would be able to access inexpensive labor in Mexico to penetrate the U.S. and Canadian markets in a straightforward North American free trade agreement.[4] Similarly, the United States and Canada would lack the leverage in Mexico that Japan enjoys in Asia to ensure that U.S. and Canadian sales of technology-intensive goods in Mexico match U.S. and Canadian purchases of low-technology goods from Mexico. Overall, in the combined North American-Southeast/East Asian market, a significant imbalance of market opportunities would exist between U.S./Canadian and Japanese MNCs.

The United States might be able to cope with such a market access disadvantage if it enjoyed a superior competitive position in technology and human resources, but it does not. Such a turn of events would thus exacerbate the adjustments imposed by low Mexican wages on U.S. industrial workers. The United States faces some hard choices.

A VIABLE NORTH AMERICAN ECONOMIC COMMUNITY

As discussed in Chapter 6, the logical alternative for the United States appears to be to seek preferential access to the Mexican market. Because strict rules of origin would not suffice, this entails asking the Mexicans to take administrative steps in areas such as investment access and screening, which at first pass appears to weaken the MFN principle and the GATT.

Also, owing to the disparity between Mexican and U.S. wages, the United States would have to manage the growth of Mexican imports in some sensitive sectors and perhaps limit imports from other developing countries.

If policymakers balk at these options, they risk a firestorm of opposition to free trade among industrial workers during the first severe recession following the inauguration of an agreement with Mexico.

Yet, these kinds of actions could weaken U.S. standing in the GATT. Whether they would depends on how they are presented. Let us reconsider the conundrum.

> The United States seeks to open trade with Mexico for political/security reasons and to counter the advantages of access to inexpensive labor that the EC and Japan enjoy in their regions.

> The United States finds talks with Mexico so important because the fissures separating U.S. and Japanese/EC approaches to trade policy block progress in the GATT that would make many issues in the trade talks with Mexico moot.

> The United States should find talks with Mexico troublesome in part because differences in Japanese and U.S. approaches to trade policy disadvantage the United States in the process of creating preferential regional trading blocs in North America and Asia.

> Consequently, the United States is faced with the necessity of seeking preferential access in Mexico—seeking two-tier MFN—and limiting third country access to U.S. markets.

Does the latter course weaken the GATT? Perhaps not. Two-tier MFN and discrimination toward third parties is exactly what participants in an economic community practice. Unlike members of a simple free trade area, Japan and EC states afford terms of access to the members of their informal and formal trading blocs that transcend tariff preferences.

The bottom line is that the United States cannot limit its options in North America to a simple free trade area and tariff preferences when the participants in the other two major trading blocs are not similarly constrained. There are some aspects of atomistic capitalism that cannot be practiced alone!

In the end, the United States is not being pushed toward GATT-inconsistent actions as much as it is being pushed toward creating a single North American market with a common external regime that extends beyond tariffs—a North American Economic Community. In a transparent and fairly benign sense, this is what is emerging out of the EC 1992 process; in a less transparent and less benign (more predatory) sense, this is the net effect of trading relationships emerging in Asia from Japanese investment and foreign aid dominance there.

The evolution of a North American Economic Community would give U.S., Canadian and Mexican efforts to obtain an equitable share of market opportunities in the North American-East/Southeast Asian market more effectiveness and international legitimacy.

It would put such efforts on a plane equivalent to the EC trade policy. With such an organized trading bloc, the United States, as the lead partner, would be in a much better position to pursue its model of atomistic market capitalism within North America. It would be better insulated from the predation of Japanese syndicate capitalism. It would be in a stronger position to lever concessions in bilateral and multilateral negotiations.

RAISING THE STAKES?

As discussed in Chapter 6, the creation of a North American free trade area poses considerable challenges. Raising the stakes to the creation of a North American Economic Community seems at first to be even more daunting. However, it is important to recognize four issues.

First, the United States cannot be guaranteed gains from free trade with Mexico without the conformation of Mexican economic and legal institutions to U.S. and Canadian norms and without preferential access to the Mexican market.

Second, conformation of Mexican policies requires, at a minimum, the ascendance of a trade agreement and Mexican policies to disciplines comparable to those of the Canada-U.S. FTA. As noted in Chapter 6, an agreement with Mexico, to be effective, must ultimately cut wider and deeper than the FTA.

Third, as observed in Chapter 4, under the FTA the United States and Canada are creating an economic community minus a common external policy and governing institution. The process of creating a free trade area, when foreign investment and many elements of domestic policy and regulation are on the table in addition to tariffs, takes negotiators a very long way toward creating a formal economic community.

Fourth, as discussed above, provisions for preferential access would be easier to implement, more legitimate in the GATT and more useful in bilateral and multilateral negotiations if the United States, Canada and Mexico established a *formal* economic community.

An economic community would require stronger commitments about the harmonization of policies than is required by a free trade area. It would necessitate the creation of a central governing body. Meeting the latter requirement would create acute political discomfort in Washington, Ottawa and Mexico City, as it would raise well-founded and emotional concerns about political sovereignty.

However, it is important to be clear that creating a North American free trade area that encompasses disciplines for foreign investment, domestic policies and regulations and preferential access beyond duty free trade creates the key elements of an economic community. Without a formal commitment to create an economic community, a free trade area lacks the legitimacy and negotiating clout that accompanies formal status in the GATT; the more efficient and less painful management to be achieved through the processes of a central governing body; and the competitive benefits to be obtained from a common external policy that serves the competitive interests of an integrated North American economy.

FIRST STEPS

Creating a North American free trade area would take many years, and the United States would be at risk in any agreement.

- The United States would afford Mexico, through tariff cuts and dispute settlement, preferential and assured access to the U.S. market well before the processes of economic reform in Mexico are wholly conceived or completed.

- Adjustment pressures could easily outstrip the flexibility of U.S. labor markets, creating unacceptable downward pressures on industrial wages.

- The provisions regarding preferential access for U.S. and Canadian goods in Mexico, by the nature of the administrative discretion involved, would not be as precise and enforceable as the preferences Mexico would receive through tariff cuts and dispute settlement.

- Beyond concerns about preferential access, it is important to recognize that the process of economic reform will extend into the administrations of President Salinas's successors. After the United States has granted Mexico preferential access, the potential for backsliding or the evolution of a Japanese- or French-style approach to managing a market economy cannot be dismissed, given Mexico's parastatal past. Should a less market-oriented administration or an administration with a more *dirigiste* orientation follow the Salinas Administration in 1994 or 2000, U.S. expectations about market access and the nature of competition from Mexico could go unfulfilled. U.S. business and labor could then fall prey to aggressive industrial targeting.

- In extending market access to other Latin American countries, the United States cannot afford the complications or inefficiencies that could be imposed by a hub-and-spoke system of bilateral agreements. It certainly cannot afford to absorb all of the adjustment costs of extending enhanced market opportunities to these nations. The United States should seek a commitment from Mexico, prior to granting it any further preferential access, to be a full partner in extending and defining enhanced market access for other Latin American nations.

At the outset of any agreement, the United States, Canada and Mexico should agree on fairly precise modalities and timetables for conforming Mexican economic policies and practices to U.S. and Canadian norms and expectations; setting up safeguard and adjustment provisions for vulnerable industries in the United States, Canada and Mexico; establishing preferences for North American products within each of the three participating economies; and defining accession provisions for other Latin American countries.

The implementation process should be seen as encompassing three sets of elements.

First, the elimination of tariffs and nontariff impediments to the efficient allocation of continental resources would be at the core of any agreement. This includes the full range of issues addressed by the FTA—the scope of national treatment, rules of origin, quotas and other border measures, safeguards, standards, procurement, subsidies and dumping, investment, business and financial services, intellectual property, dispute settlement, and sectoral issues.

The agreement should also include other issues to ensure a level playing field—environmental and workplace standards, antitrust and other measures necessary to ensure the general ascendancy of Mexican economic practices to the norms of transparency and nondiscrimination expected of a partner in an economic community.

In addressing these issues, the United States needs safeguards against backsliding by future Mexican governments and the evolution of *dirigiste* policies that might compromise U.S. interests.

Second, transitional provisions would be key to cushioning adjustment for both economies. The phasing in of increased access to U.S./Canadian and Mexican markets must be consistent with the adjustment needs of the workers and industries involved.

Third, the provision of preferential access for the United States and Canada should be seen as a beginning to the process of creating a formal economic community. Competitive pressures from Japan and the EC, as well as the leverage to be gained in international negotiations, mandate that the United States, Canada and Mexico seek the competitive advantages and legitimacy of concerted action that the Japanese and EC states are obtaining in their economic communities in Asia and Europe.

NOTES

1. It may be argued that the Europeans, in particular the French, have evolved yet a third model—*social market capitalism.* Although a special case of *syndicate capitalism,* it may show greater concern for social goals.

2. This is why, for example, the EC clings to selectivity in the application of safeguards and will not entertain meaningful disciplines on industrial subsidies in the Uruguay Round.

3. Again, as discussed below, this results from fundamental differences between U.S. and Japanese approaches to trade policies that place the United States at a disadvantage as regional markets emerge.

4. Meanwhile, Europe is evolving into a market of three concentric circles—a single market among the generally more advanced EC countries, free trade in the classic sense (the absence of tariffs, quantitative restrictions and onerous border measures) with the advanced Western European

countries outside the EC and enhanced access to the EC market for Eastern European neighbors. This setup requires EC countries to accept the imports of their "single market partners" and the remaining nations of Western Europe but offers them the opportunity to control imports from the "outer circle." Hence, Japanese MNCs cannot set up shop in Eastern Europe and be assured access to the EC market. With the development progress of Eastern Europe, the boundaries between the inner circle and the outer circle may become more perforated—they could even disappear with EC membership for Eastern bloc countries. However, this is years away.

APPENDIX A
The Canada-U.S. Free Trade Agreement

The Canada-U.S. Free Trade Agreement, which came into force January 1, 1989, is a comprehensive arrangement covering trade in goods and services and direct investment flows. It phases out tariffs, liberalizes many nontariff policies and practices, and imposes a standstill on most other nontariff measures. With regard to the latter, it establishes an ambitious negotiating agenda for achieving further progress. Most notable are the efforts to define common rules for subsidies and dumping, product standards and services.

This appendix reviews the institutional and economic forces that caused Canada and the United States to negotiate the FTA and summarizes its principal provisions.[1]

HISTORICAL BACKGROUND

The idea of a U.S.-Canadian trade area has a long history. When Britain ended imperial preferences in the late 1840s, Canada sought improved access to the U.S. market. From 1854 to 1866, the two countries engaged in duty free trade in natural resource products under the Reciprocal Trade Agreement.[2] The United States terminated the arrangement in 1866 partly in response to the Cayley-Galt tariffs of 1858–59, which greatly increased the protection afforded Canadian manufacturers, and British preference for the Confederacy during the Civil War. Several efforts to negotiate a broader agreement failed, including an 1874 agreement, rejected by the U.S. Senate, and a 1911 agreement, rejected by Canadian voters in a national election. Meanwhile, Canada's National Policy of 1879 became firmly entrenched. Its key elements included still higher tariffs to promote manufacturing and a transcontinental railway to link Canadian centers of economic activity east to west. After World War II, Canada encountered severe balance-of-payments problems; one solution considered was a preferential trading arrangement with the United States. In 1948, a free trade area emerged as the likely outcome of secret negotiations. However, Canada's payments problems subsided, and Prime Minister Mackenzie King developed second thoughts about such close ties with the United States.

During the 1960s and 1970s, the concept received continued attention from Canadian business leaders, academics and government officials. This reflected their attraction to secure, free access to the large U.S. market as a means of improving Canadian manufacturing productivity and for spreading product development costs in high-technology activities. However, Canadians have viewed growing commercial ties with the United States with much ambivalence, reflecting concerns about the pervasive influence of U.S. investment, culture and politics on their economy and national life.

CANADIAN GOALS

Canada's substantial natural resource endowment, coupled with a small domestic market, has encouraged Canadian specialization in resource-based exports. These industries, being capital-intensive, attracted significant foreign investment. Also, high tariffs encouraged foreign manufacturers to establish plants in Canada to service its market. Although U.S.-Canadian trade has generally reflected underlying comparative advantages, trade and specialization have been reduced by trade barriers, as capital flows in part substituted for trade flows.

During the 1950s and most of the 1960s, Canada was content to pursue trade liberalization through the General Agreement on Tariffs and Trade.[3] It was open to U.S. investment and had a minimum of industrial policies for intervening in market processes. In the 1970s and early 1980s, Canadians became more concerned about the influence of U.S. multinational corporations, and many perceived increased economic integration with the United States as fostering cultural and social integration.[4] By implementing a series of industrial policies, including screening of new foreign investment,[5] the Trudeau government sought to reduce Canada's dependence on the United States—the so-called Third Option—and to improve Canadian competitiveness in nonextractive activities. The latter goal was often defined as increasing productivity in manufacturing. These efforts were not a great success. Although U.S. ownership of Canadian industry declined, the U.S. share of Canada's trade did not fall; in 1987, Canadian manufacturing productivity was about 75 percent of U.S. levels, the same as in 1966.[6] Canada's foreign investment policies, as well as its National Energy Program, drew strong criticism from Washington and U.S. firms operating in Canada.

Meanwhile, in the United States, adjustment problems and large trade deficits gave impetus to protectionist measures. U.S. actions in industries important to Canada, such as steel, lumber and fish products, raised concerns about the security of Canada's continued access to the U.S. market. Ultimately, a consensus emerged among Canadian advocates of free trade that growth in international resource markets would no longer sustain adequate domestic growth and that the competitiveness of Canadian manufacturing must be improved.[7] Foreign nontariff barriers and the threat of new barriers, especially in the United States, were identified as among the principal obstacles to restructuring Canadian industry.[8] Beginning in late 1982, nationalist policies were gradually abandoned, and in 1984, Canada undertook preliminary sectoral talks with the United States. Subsequently, the two governments agreed to explore a comprehensive agreement. Canada's objectives were to:

- secure access to the U.S. market by limiting Canadian exposure to U.S. trade remedy laws—e.g., exemption from U.S. safeguard actions and a joint definition of a countervailable subsidy;

- enhance market access by eliminating tariffs and liberalizing nontariff measures—e.g., federal and state procurement, product standards and licensing, patents and copyrights, and the Jones Act;

- enshrine these gains in a strong agreement with an effective dispute settlement mechanism; and

- maintain independence of action in cultural industries and the regulation of foreign investment in some sensitive sectors.[9]

U.S. OBJECTIVES

Since the late 1970s, as tariffs have become less significant in multilateral trade negotiations, U.S. attention has increasingly turned to the limitations or absence of GATT rules for agriculture, domestic subsidies, intellectual property, government procurement, trade-related investment issues, and services. When negotiations began in 1986, a bilateral agreement with Canada was seen as potentially providing a model for GATT talks in these areas. Also, it was seen by U.S. officials as providing a lever in the multilateral process by indicating to Japan, the EC and others that the United States is prepared to pursue other avenues if the Uruguay Round does not deliver tangible benefits.[10]

Equally important, the negotiations offered an opportunity to eliminate higher Canadian tariffs[11] and to enshrine improvements in the bilateral trade and investment climate achieved in recent years. The United States sought assurances that Canada would not reinstate cumbersome screening and performance requirements on U.S. direct investment or limit U.S. access to Canadian energy. Other issues high on the U.S. agenda were:

- federal and provincial procurement; discrimination by Canadian wholesalers and retailers against U.S. liquor, wine and beer; barriers to U.S. exports of poultry, eggs, dairy products, and meats; seasonal tariffs on fresh fruits and vegetables; and product standards and testing;

- Canadian subsidies and duty remissions benefits for foreign firms undertaking to source or produce in Canada—e.g., Canadian remission of duties on Asian and European cars whose makers source parts or establish production facilities in Canada was seen by Americans as violating the intent of the 1965 Automotive Agreement[12];

- a comprehensive agreement on trade in services; and

- resolution of several other outstanding bilateral issues— e.g., better protection for U.S. pharmaceutical patents and copyright protection for U.S. television signals retransmitted in Canada.

PRINCIPAL PROVISIONS OF THE FTA

In the Preamble and Chapter 1, the two governments state their political commitments to create a free trade area, liberalize investment flows and trade in services, and resolve commercial disputes according to mutually agreed upon rules in a jointly administered, bilateral framework.

Trade in Goods

The FTA will phase out all *tariffs* within 10 years, and it reinforces the GATT principle of *national treatment. Duty remission and drawback programs* also will be phased out.[13]

Rules of origin for duty free treatment require that components imported from third countries be incorporated into other goods or transformed in physically or commercially significant ways. In most cases, this requirement is met when a production process results in a change in tariff classification or, as back up, 50 percent U.S.-Canadian value added.[14]

Import quotas and *export controls* are prohibited unless grandfathered or in accordance with GATT rules. On the import side, this establishes more of a standstill, prohibiting new measures, than it signals progress.[15] The GATT exclusion is important in agriculture, the sector with most of the quantitative restrictions. Export controls are allowed in the event of shortages, but supplies must be allocated on the basis of consumption patterns for the previous three years.[16] Coupled with prohibitions on *dual pricing of exports* and *export taxes*, this should assure American consumers access to Canadian *energy* at prices similar to those paid by Canadian consumers under comparable commercial circumstances.

The FTA establishes rules for bilateral and global *safeguard actions*. Until December 31, 1998, either country may respond to serious injury resulting from FTA tariff reductions by restoring duties up to three years.[17] The United States and Canada will exempt each other from global safeguard actions, *except* in cases where the other country is a substantial source of injury (more than 5 to 10 percent of imports). In any case, imports from Canada (the United States) may not be reduced below their trend "over a reasonable base period with allowance for growth."[18]

Each country will continue to define its own *product standards*, which may be stricter in one country or the other; however, the two federal governments agree to avoid unnecessary impediments to trade. This does not apply to existing measures. But the two governments are committed to harmonizing standards, where appropriate, so that products do not have to be made differently to be sold in both countries.

The two federal governments agree to recognize each other's testing facilities and certification bodies. These commitments are not binding on private standards setting bodies—e.g., Underwriters Laboratories—but the two governments agree to encourage these entities to harmonize standards and make testing procedures compatible.

In agriculture, food and related products (e.g., seeds, pesticides and veterinary drugs), the United States and Canada will seek an "open border" by completely harmonizing technical regulations and inspection procedures.

The FTA lowers the threshold on *government procurement* covered by the GATT Procurement Code from $171,000 to $25,000 and requires more transparent bidding procedures. Generally, these provisions only apply to goods and have no impact on the practices of states and provinces.

The United States and Canada will undertake negotiations to define common rules for *subsidies and dumping* within five to seven years; meanwhile existing national laws will apply. Changes in U.S. (Canadian) laws will apply to Canada (United

States) only if Canada (the United States) is specifically named and such changes are consistent with the GATT and general intent of the FTA.

To ensure that the U.S. International Trade Commission and the Department of Commerce (Canadian Department of National Revenue and International Trade Tribunal) are free to apply these laws objectively, namely without political influence, judicial review of their findings will be replaced by binding review by binational panels. These panels will examine whether agency findings are "in accordance with the antidumping or countervailing duty law of the importing country."[19] Under extraordinary circumstances, these panel decisions may be appealed to a binational panel of retired judges. In any case, the final outcome is binding.

Sectoral Provisions

In *agriculture,* the trade and overproduction problems created by export subsidies and farm support programs require multilateral solutions; however, the FTA takes some positive steps. Export subsidies in bilateral trade are prohibited. Canada will remove import restrictions on U.S. wheat, oats and barley when U.S. support levels are lowered to Canadian levels. Both countries are now exempt from each other's red meat import laws. However, U.S. import restrictions on sugar-containing products and Canadian quotas on poultry and eggs are moderated only slightly, and both countries' dairy programs are largely unaffected. Generally, U.S. *wine and liquor* will receive national treatment in Canada by January 1995.[20]

Under the *Automotive Agreement of 1965,* Canada essentially affords duty free treatment to vehicles and original equipment parts made by firms that assemble one car in Canada for each car sold there and achieve value added in Canada equal to 60 percent of sales there. Among passenger car manufacturers, only General Motors, Ford, Chrysler, and Volvo meet these requirements. In contrast, the United States requires only that Canadian-based manufacturers meet a 50 percent U.S.-Canadian content requirement. The FTA will phase out tariffs on all bilateral trade in automotive products (including replacement parts and the U.S.-Canadian products of Asian and European producers), meeting a very strict 50 percent U.S.-Canadian content rule. Unlike the old U.S. content rule, overhead and other indirect costs may not be counted.[21]

Cultural industries—namely, the production and distribution of books, magazines, newspapers, films, recordings, and broadcasting—are exempt from most provisions of the FTA. In response to Canadian actions, the United States "may take actions of equivalent commercial effect."[22] Canada will afford copyright protection to retransmitted U.S. broadcast signals.

Services

The U.S. and Canadian governments will afford each other's nonfinancial *business services* national treatment, right of establishment and guaranteed access to local distribution systems, with the exception of medical and legal services, childcare, basic telecommunications, transportation, and government services. The two governments "shall encourage the mutual recognition of licensing and certification requirements," which they have agreed should relate principally to competence and "shall not have the purpose or effect of discriminatorily impairing or restraining access of nationals of the other party to such licensing or certification."[23] These commitments do not apply to subsidies, government procurement or existing nonconforming practices— hence, most of the benefits are prospective. Sectoral annexes apply these principles to architecture, enhanced telecommunications services and tourism. The two governments are committed to negotiations to remove the discriminatory effects of existing regulations in other sectors.

Financial services are covered in a separate chapter. Since 1986, regulators in Ottawa and Ontario have taken major steps to give U.S. firms better market access. These are codified in the FTA and provide U.S. commercial banks and securities firms with substantial new freedom to diversify and expand in Canada. For example, U.S. financial institutions are now able to buy 100 percent of a Canadian securities dealer, U.S. firms may fully participate in Ontario and Quebec securities markets, and U.S. commercial banks are freed from the 16 percent ceiling on foreign holdings of Canadian bank assets. In the United States, Canadian firms already enjoy considerable freedom in these areas. To the extent the United States and Canada continue to deregulate and restructure their financial sectors, the two governments will seek mutually assured benefits.

Should the U.S. government amend the Glass-Steagall Act, Canadian financial institutions would be afforded the same benefits as their U.S. counterparts. The United States is not similarly bound under existing agreements to extend such benefits to other countries.

Investment

Chapter 16 establishes a comprehensive regime regarding the treatment of foreign direct investment outside the financial sector.

Once established, the United States and Canada will provide national treatment for each other's businesses. The FTA prohibits minimum national equity requirements, and firms and individuals may not be forced to sell their assets on account of their nationality. The United States agrees not to screen new Canadian direct investments and acquisitions, even it establishes a general screening program in the future. Canada reserves the right to screen direct acquisitions of only its financial institutions and largest industrial corporations. Both countries agree not to seek performance undertakings from foreign investors that could directly distort trade—i.e., requirements for domestic sourcing, import substitution or export goals.

Exempt from the provisions of the investment chapter are U.S. restrictions on foreign investment in the communications and atomic energy sectors and Canadian restrictions in the communications, oil and gas, uranium, and cultural industries.

Dispute Settlement

A Canada-United States Trade Commission[24] will mediate most disputes.[25] When problems arise, the first step will be consultations. Should these fail, either country may ask the Commission to take up the issue or seek resolution through the GATT. If the Commission fails to achieve a mutually satisfactory resolution within 30 days, a panel of five experts may be established to make recommendations, and generally their findings will be published. "Whenever possible, the resolution shall be non-implementation or removal of a measure not conforming with this Agreement . . . or, failing such a resolution, compensation."[26] Binding arbitration is available if both parties agree. All disputed safeguard actions will be subject to binding arbitration.

CONCLUSIONS

The FTA makes a good start in creating a fully integrated U.S.-Canadian market for goods, services and capital. Focusing on trade in goods, the elimination of tariffs, prohibitions on new import restrictions, export subsidies and embargoes, as well as constraints on safeguard actions, will provide many of the efficiency benefits of duty free trade. The mutual recognition of product testing, a lower threshold for purchases covered by the GATT Procurement Code, more transparent bidding procedures for government procurement, the prohibition on investment performance requirements directly affecting trade, and binational review of national subsidy and dumping determinations also signal important progress. Turning to business services, guarantees of national treatment and right of establishment, as well as the joint commitment to avoid new discriminatory licensing, certification and regulatory procedures should provide service firms with the kind of certainty about continued market access necessary to undertake investments on both sides of the border. The provisions regarding foreign investment and financial services will bring the United States and Canada many of the benefits of an integrated capital market.

Neither country achieved all its goals; however, each can claim important progress. Canada has clearly enhanced its market access, and the new rules for safeguard actions, which are now subject to binding arbitration, should give Canada more secure access to the U.S. market. The dispute settlement mechanism for subsidies and dumping should help establish confidence that each country is applying relevant trade laws objectively; however, the negotiation of joint rules remains a key Canadian goal. Canada maintains considerable latitude to promote its cultural industries and to screen acquisitions of its financial institutions and largest industrial companies.

The United States achieved its most important goals: elimination of higher Canadian tariffs, comprehensive agreements for direct investment and business services, improved market access in the financial sector, and the resolution of several narrower issues—e.g., improved protection for pharmaceutical patents, copyright protection for retransmitted television signals and better market access for wine and liquor.

As in all negotiations, both governments had to consider the domestic politics of ratification; hence, the FTA will have relatively little impact on certain discriminatory practices. Examples include U.S. quotas on sugar-containing products and Canadian quotas on dairy and poultry, and the FTA's failure to include government purchases of services and state and provincial procurement practices.

Although a great deal has been achieved, it is important to recognize that many of the benefits of the FTA are prospective. The agreement establishes an extensive negotiating agenda in areas such as product standards, business and financial services, and dumping and subsidy rules. As much as they are creating a free trade area, the United States and Canada are now committed to creating a single market and economic community less a common external trade regime and central governing body.

NOTES

1. This appendix was adapted from Peter Morici, "The Canada-U.S. Free-Trade Agreement," *International Trade Journal* (Summer 1989). Adapted with permission.

2. The Reciprocal Free Trade Agreement, part of the Elgin-Marcy Treaty of 1854, established duty free trade between the United States and the British-North American Territories of Canada (present day Ontario and Quebec), New Brunswick, Nova Scotia, Prince Edward Island, and Newfoundland in agricultural and forest products; ores and metals; dairy products; animal, fish and kindred products; and only a few manufactures (dyestuff and rags). This covered about 90 and 55 percent of Canadian and U.S. exports, respectively. See Anna Guthrie, "A Brief History of Canadian-American Reciprocity," in Sperry Lea, *A Canada-U.S. Free Trade Arrangement: Survey of Possible Characteristics* (Washington and Montreal: Canadian-American Committee, 1963), Appendix A, pp. 83–92; J.L. Granatstein, "Free Trade Between Canada and the United States: The Issue That Will Not Go Away" in Dennis Stairs and Gilbert R. Winham, eds., *The Politics of Canada's Economic Relationship With the United States* (Toronto: University of Toronto Press for the Royal Commission on the Economic Development Prospects for Canada, 1985), pp. 11–54.

3. The most important exception was the Automotive Agreement of 1965; it established duty-free bilateral trade in new vehicles and original equipment parts.

4. In discussing expanding bilateral commercial ties, the 1970 Canadian White Paper on foreign policy stated: "While such developments should be beneficial for Canada's growth, the constant danger that sovereignty, independence and cultural identity may be impaired will require a conscious effort on Canada's part to keep the whole situation under control." External Affairs, *Foreign Policy for Canadians* (Ottawa, 1970), p. 24.

5. From foreign firms seeking to establish new businesses or acquire Canadian companies, the Foreign Investment Review Agency obtained undertakings to source in Canada, meet export goals, employ Canadian managers, appoint Canadian directors, establish R&D facilities in Canada, and grant Canadian subsidiaries world product mandates, as well as other commitments to increase the benefits of foreign investment to Canada.

Other tools of industrial policy included: extensive financial incentives to promote increased natural resource processing, secondary manufacturing, regional development, and technology-intensive activities; the National Energy Program; aggressive federal and provincial purchasing policies; efforts to steer private procurement for major resource projects to Canadian suppliers; and duty remission programs to encourage foreign manufacturers to source components or locate plants in Canada. See Peter Morici, Arthur Smith and Sperry Lea, *Canadian Industrial Policy* (Washington: National Planning Association, 1982), Chapter 4.

6. Total factor productivity—see Someshwar Rao, "U.S.-Canada Productivity Gap, Scale Economies, and the Gains from Free Trade" (Ottawa: Economic Council of Canada Discussion Paper No. 357 September 1988).

7. Most notable in this regard were a series of government discussion papers and reports culminating in the report of the *Royal Commission on the Economic Union and Development Prospects for Canada* (Ottawa: Ministry of Supply and Services, 1985).

8. "The threat of [U.S.] countervail has proven to be a major deterrent to investment in Canada"—Minister for External Trade and Secretary of State for External Affairs, *Canadian Trade Negotiations* (Ottawa: Department of External Affairs, 1985), p. 26.

9. Ibid., pp. 3–4 and 25–27.

10. According to then Treasury Secretary James Baker: "This agreement is also a lever to achieve more open trade. Other nations are forced to recognize that the United States will devise ways to expand trade—with or without them. If they choose not to open markets, they will not reap the benefits." *The International Economy* (January/February 1988), p. 41.

11. At the conclusion of the Tokyo Round tariff cuts in 1987, average Canadian tariffs on U.S. imports were 9 to 10 percent; the comparable figures for the United States were 4 to 5 percent. Ambassador Clayton Yeutter, *Testimony Before the Senate Committee on U.S.-Canada Trade Negotiations* (April 11, 1986), p. 3.

12. See footnote 5.

13. Also, for goods made in *Free Trade Zones*, duties must be paid on third country components whether final products are sold in Canada or the United States.

14. Fifty percent content is required for automotive products.
   Apparel made from fabrics imported from third countries will only qualify for duty free trade up to the following annual limits:

	Nonwoolen	Woolen
	(mills. of square-yard equivalent)	
Canadian exports	50	6
U.S. exports	10.5	1.1

15. The FTA ends Canadian embargoes on used aircraft and used automobiles and U.S. embargoes on lottery materials. It prohibits the reimposition of U.S. restrictions on unprocessed uranium and eliminates Canada's requirement that uranium be processed before being exported.

16. Subject to GATT disciplines, both countries may restrict exports of logs, and Quebec and the Atlantic Provinces may restrict exports of unprocessed fish.

17. In each industry, tariffs may be restored only once. The single exception is tariffs on fresh fruits and vegetables; these may be reinstated during periods of depressed market conditions for up to 20 years.

18. FTA Article 1102, paragraph 4.b.

19. FTA Article 1904, paragraph 2.

20. Canadian practices with regard to foreign beer have been found in violation of the GATT; the United States and European Community are awaiting Canada's response.

21. Under the Automotive Agreement, the United States admits only duty free cars assembled in Canada and original equipment parts made there. In contrast, Canada admits duty free these products made in the United States and the offshore imports of companies meeting Canada's fairly strict content requirements; as noted, among manufacturers of passenger cars, only General Motors, Chrysler, Ford, and Volvo have qualified for these benefits. Hence, by meeting Canada's strict content requirements, these producers may bring captive imports into Canada without paying a 9.2 percent duty—a decided advantage over Japanese, Korean and other foreign companies.

    When Volkswagen and Asian manufacturers began establishing plants in the United States, partly in response to U.S. protectionist pressures, Canada offered duty remission on their vehicle imports in return for purchasing Canadian parts for export or for establishing significant production facilities in Canada. This significantly shifted the incentives for foreign manufacturers as to the choice of plant locations between the two countries in favor of Canada. Under the FTA, Canada agrees to phase out duty remission benefits. The three major North American manufacturers and Volvo may continue to meet the old Canadian requirements and bring captive imports into Canada duty free. Canada agrees not to extend the latter benefits to other foreign passenger vehicle manufactures.

22. FTA Article 2005, paragraph 2.

23. FTA Article 1403.

24. The ministers responsible for international trade, or their designated representative, serve as their country's principal representatives.

25. Disputes concerning subsidy/countervailing duties and antidumping duties are subject to a separate binding dispute settlement mechanism. Disputes relating to financial services will be resolved through consultations between the Departments of Finance and Treasury. The decisions of Investment Canada with respect to acquisitions are final and may not be appealed through the FTA dispute settlement procedure.

26. FTA Article 1807, paragraph 8.

APPENDIX B
Distribution of U.S. Trade with Canada, 1979 and 1989

SITC		Imports 1979	Imports 1989	Exports 1979	Exports 1989
			(Percent)		
0	Food and Live Animals	3.5	4.0	4.1	2.6
1	Beverages and Tobacco	0.9	0.7	0.1	0.1
2	Crude Materials, Inedible, except Minerals	15.9	9.4	5.3	3.1
3	Mineral Fuels, Lubricants and Related Products	14.3	9.1	4.9	2.2
32	Coal, Coke and Briquettes	0.1	0.1	3.1	1.0
33	Petroleum and Related Products	6.5	5.8	1.8	0.9
34	Gas, Natural and Manufactured	7.6	2.5	*	0.1
4	Animal and Vegetable Oils, Fats, Waxes	*	0.1	0.1	0.1
5	Chemicals and Related Products, NES	6.4	4.6	6.6	5.6
51	Organic Chemicals	1.3	0.7	1.4	1.3
52	Inorganic Chemicals	2.3	1.4	0.8	0.6
53	Dyeing, Tanning, Coloring Materials	*	0.1	0.3	0.3
54	Medicinal, Pharmaceutical Products	0.1	0.1	0.4	0.4
55	Essential Oils, Perfumes, Soaps, Cleansers	0.1	0.2	0.3	0.3
56	Fertilizers, Manufactured	2.2	0.9	0.3	0.3
57	Explosives, Pyrotechnic Products	0.1	0.6	*	0.9
58	Artificial Resins and Plastics, Ethers	0.2	0.4	1.6	0.6
59	Chemical Materials and Products	0.2	0.2	1.3	0.9
6	Manufactured Goods Classified by Mat.	19.0	19.2	12.0	7.9
61	Leather and Furskins	0.1	*	0.2	0.1
62	Rubber Manufactures	0.8	0.9	0.9	0.6
63	Cord and Food Manufactures	1.0	0.8	0.3	0.3
64	Paper, Paperboard, Articles of Pulp	7.5	7.2	1.2	1.0
65	Textile Yarns, Fabrics, NES	0.1	0.4	2.0	0.9
66	Nonmetallic Mineral Manufactures, NES	1.0	0.8	1.5	0.9
67	Iron and Steel	2.5	1.9	1.9	0.8
68	Nonferrous Metals	4.3	5.4	1.3	1.4
69	Manufactures of Metals	1.8	1.7	2.8	1.7
7	Machinery and Transport Equipment	34.2	44.4	57.8	44.5
71	Power Gen. Machinery and Equipment	2.8	3.2	5.9	3.9
72	Machinery Specific by Industry	2.8	1.8	7.2	3.3
73	Metalworking Machinery	0.3	0.3	0.8	0.5
74	Industrial Machinery and Equip., NES	1.8	2.0	6.0	3.7
75	Office Machines and Data Processors	1.0	1.9	2.6	3.4
76	Telecommunications	0.8	1.1	1.1	1.1
77	Electrical Machinery and Parts	1.4	2.8	3.7	5.0
78	Road Vehicles	21.9	29.2	27.9	21.3
79	Other Transportation Equipment	1.5	2.2	2.5	2.2
8	Misc. Manufactured Articles	2.7	4.1	6.1	5.8
81	Plumbing, Heating, Lighting Fixtures	*	0.1	0.2	0.2
82	Furniture and Parts Thereof	0.9	1.3	0.4	0.4
83	Travel Goods, Handbags	*	*	*	*
84	Articles of Apparel, Clothing Accessories	0.1	0.3	0.2	0.1
85	Footwear	0.1	0.1	*	*
87	Scientific, Controlling Instruments	0.3	0.5	1.7	1.6
88	Photographic Equip., Watches, Clocks	0.2	0.2	0.8	0.5
89	Misc. Manufactured Articles, NES	1.1	1.6	2.8	2.9
9	Commodities and Transactions, NES	3.1	4.4	2.9	28.2
	Total in Millions of U.S. Dollars	$38,459.8	$88,543.3	$31,217.8	$74,604.5

* = less than 0.05 percent.

Source: OECD, *Foreign Trade by Commodities: Series C.*

National Planning Association

NPA is an independent, private, nonprofit, nonpolitical organization that carries on research and policy formulation in the public interest. NPA was founded during the Great Depression of the 1930s when conflicts among the major economic groups—business, labor, agriculture—threatened to paralyze national decisionmaking on the critical issues confronting American society. It was dedicated to the task of getting these diverse groups to work together to narrow areas of controversy and broaden areas of agreement as well as to map out specific programs for action in the best traditions of a functioning democracy. Such democratic and decentralized planning, NPA believes, involves the development of effective governmental and private policies and programs not only by official agencies but also through the independent initiative and cooperation of the main private sector groups concerned.

To this end, NPA brings together influential and knowledgeable leaders from business, labor, agriculture, and the applied and academic professions to serve on policy committees. These committees identify emerging problems confronting the nation at home and abroad and seek to develop and agree upon policies and programs for coping with them. The research and writing for these committees are provided by NPA's professional staff and, as required, by outside experts.

In addition, NPA's professional staff undertakes research through its central or "core" program designed to provide data and ideas for policymakers and planners in government and the private sector. These activities include research on national goals and priorities, productivity and economic growth, welfare and dependency problems, employment and human resource needs, and technological change; analyses and forecasts of changing international realities and their implications for U.S. policies; and analyses of important new economic, social and political realities confronting American society.

In developing its staff capabilities, NPA has increasingly emphasized two related qualifications. First is the interdisciplinary knowledge required to understand the complex nature of many real-life problems. Second is the ability to bridge the gap between theoretical or highly technical research and the practical needs of policymakers and planners in government and the private sector.

Through its committees and its core program, NPA addresses a wide range of issues. Not all of the NPA Trustees or committee members are in full agreement with all that is contained in these publications unless such endorsement is specifically stated.

117

NPA Committee on Changing International Realities

The Committee on Changing International Realities was established by the National Planning Association in 1975 to improve understanding of the challenges confronting the U.S. private and public sectors in the international economy. In accordance with NPA's practice, the CIR is composed of leaders from industry, finance, agriculture, labor, and the academic and applied professions. By bringing together key representatives from such diverse concerns and perspectives, the Committee is uniquely qualified to aid in the formulation of effective economic and foreign policies.

The CIR undertakes a continuing program with three primary purposes: (1) to give private sector leaders the opportunity to discuss in an informal atmosphere, and with public policymakers, the challenges and problems facing them in the international economy; (2) to interpret the changes in the international environment that may affect U.S. private sector interests or provide new opportunities; and (3) to encourage the formulation of better public policies by sponsoring nonpartisan research studies on the factors affecting U.S. competitiveness and international economic interests.

In recent years, the CIR has focused on the challenges to U.S. competitiveness posed by Japan and the newly industrializing countries; European plans to form an internal market by 1992; the growth of regional trading blocs; the tensions between global corporations and nation-states; changing U.S. relations with and interests in Mexico and other developing countries; strains in the international financial system; and the consequences of macroeconomic policies for U.S. trade performance.

The Committee meets twice a year to discuss, with experts in the field, pressing national and international issues. At these meetings it also focuses on subjects to be researched, reviews outlines and drafts of studies under way and considers their policy implications. Detailed guidance of the CIR's research program is carried on by subcommittees,

For further information about the CIR's continuing activities, please contact:

Richard S. Belous
NPA Vice President, International Affairs,
and CIR Director

National Planning Association
1424 16th Street, N.W., Suite 700
Washington, D.C. 20036
(202) 265-7685
Fax (202) 797-5516

Members of the Committee on Changing International Realities

JOHN J. SIMONE
Chair;
Group Executive,
Manufacturers Hanover
Trust Company

EDWARD J. CARLOUGH
Vice Chair;
General President, Sheet
Metal Workers' International
Association

C. MICHAEL AHO
Director of Economic Studies
and International
Trade Project, Council on
Foreign Relations, Inc.

J. ROBERT ANDERSON
Akron, Ohio

ALBERT D. ANGEL
Vice President-Public Affairs,
Merck & Co., Inc.

HANS W. BECHERER
Chairman and Chief
Executive Officer,
Deere and Company

GEORGE BECKER
International Vice President,
(Administration),
United Steelworkers of
America

JOE E. CHENOWETH
Senior Corporate Vice
President,
Intenational,
Honeywell, Inc.

J.G. CLARKE
Director and Senior Vice
President,
Exxon Corporation

DOMINIQUE CLAVEL
Senior Vice President,
Chase Manhattan Bank, N.A.

RICHARD V.L. COOPER
Ernst & Young

RICHARD N. COOPER
Maurits C. Boas Professor of
International Economics,
Center for International
Affairs, Harvard University

KENNETH W. DAM
Vice President, Law and
External Relations,
IBM Corporation

THIBAUT DE SAINT PHALLE
Chairman,
Saint Phalle International
Group

LODEWIJK deVINK
Executive Vice President and
President,
U.S. Operations,
Warner-Lambert Company

BARBARA J. EASTERLING
Executive Vice President,
Communications Workers of
America

MURRAY H. FINLEY
President Emeritus,
Amalgamated Clothing &
Textile Workers' Union;
Chairman of the Advisory
Committee, Amalgamated
Bank of New York

THEODORE GEIGER
Distinguished Research
Professor of Intersocietal
Relations,
School of Foreign Service,
Georgetown University

MYER RASHISH
President,
Rashish Associates, Inc.

ROBERT REISER
Senior Lecturer and Chief
Management Department,
Babson College

DAVIS R. ROBINSON
Partner,
LeBouef, Lamb, Leiby &
MacRae

JAMES ROSENFIELD
Managing Director,
Cambridge Energy Research
Associates

HERBERT SALZMAN
Bradford Associates

HOWARD D. SAMUEL
President, Industrial Union
Department, AFL-CIO

NATHANIEL SAMUELS
Advisory Director,
Shearson Lehman Hutton Inc.

PHILIP D. SHERMAN
Senior Vice President,
Investment Bank Sector,
Citicorp, N.A.

WINFRIED H. SPAEH
Senior General Manager,
Chief Executive, USA,
Dresdner Bank AG

HANS G. STORR
Senior Vice President and
Chief Financial Officer,
Philip Morris Companies, Inc.

ALEXANDER C. TOMLINSON
President,
Hungarian-American
Enterprise Fund

STEPHEN VEHSLAGE
Assistant General Manager of
U.S. Education,
IBM United States

JOHN T. WATSON
Administrative Director,
International Operations,
Pioneer Hi-Bred International

ROBERT A. WILSON
Vice President, Public Affairs,
Pfizer, Inc.

ALAN WM. WOLFF
Dewey, Ballantine, Bushby,
Palmer & Wood

CHARLES G. WOOTTON
Coordinator, International
Public Affairs,
Chevron Corporation

RALPH S. YOHE
Mt. Horeb, Wisconsin

EUGENE W. ZELTMANN
Manager of Trade and
Industry Associations,
GE Industry & Power
Systems Sales,
General Electric Company

NPA Publications

Trade Talks with Mexico: A Time for Realism, by Peter Morici (132 pp, 1991, $15.00), CIR #22.

Curing U.S. Health Care Ills, by Bert Seidman (1991), NAR #6.

A Time for Action: Ensuring the Stability of the U.S. Financial System, by Robert M. Dunn, Jr., and Richard S. Belous (48 pp, 1991, $5.00), NPA #251.

United Germany and the United States, by Michael A. Freney and Rebecca S. Hartley (196 pp, 1991, $17.50), CIR #21.

The Question of Saving, by Harold Rose (64 pp, 1991, $8.00), BN #38.

Taking Advantage of America's Window of Opportunity, A Statement by the Board of Trustees of the National Planning Association (16 pp, 1990, $2.50), NPA #248.

Creating a Strong Post-Cold War Economy, by Richard S. Belous (40 pp, 1990, $8.00), NPA #247.

Man and His Environment, by Harry G. Johnson, An Occasional Paper (44 pp, 1973, 1990 reprint, $8.00), BN-OP #6.

Transforming the Mexican Economy: The Salinas Sexenio, by Sidney Weintraub (92 pp, 1990, $12.00), CIR #20.

Preparing for Change: Workforce Excellence in a Turbulent Economy, Recommendations of the Committee on New American Realities (32 pp, 1990, $5.00), NAR #5.

Changing Sources of U.S. Economic Growth, 1950-2010: A Chartbook of Trends and Projections, by Nestor E. Terleckyj (76 pp, 1990, $15.00), NPA #244.

The Growth of Regional Trading Blocs in the Global Economy, ed. Richard S. Belous and Rebecca S. Hartley (168 pp, 1990, $15.00), NPA #243.

Continental Divide: The Values and Institutions of the United States and Canada, by Seymour Martin Lipset (326 pp, 1989, $13.00), CAC #59.

The Contingent Economy: The Growth of the Temporary, Part-Time and Subcontracted Workforce, by Richard S. Belous (136 pp, 1989, $15.00), NPA #239.

The 1992 Challenge from Europe: Development of the European Community's Internal Market, by Michael Calingaert (176 pp, 1988, with 1990 Foreword by the author, $15.00), NPA #237.

NPA membership is $65.00 per year, tax deductible. In addition to new NPA publications, members receive *Looking Ahead,* a quarterly journal, which is also available at the separate subscription price of $35.00. NPA members, upon request, may obtain a 30 percent discount on other publications in stock. A list of publications will be provided upon request. Quantity discounts are given.

Canada-U.S. Outlook, published quarterly by NPA, is available through a separate subscription rate of $35.00 per year.

NPA is a qualified nonprofit, charitable organization under section 501(c)(3) of the Internal Revenue Code.

NATIONAL PLANNING ASSOCIATION
1424 16th Street, N.W., Suite 700
Washington, D.C. 20036
Tel (202)265-7685 Fax (202)797-5516